The 1995 Complete

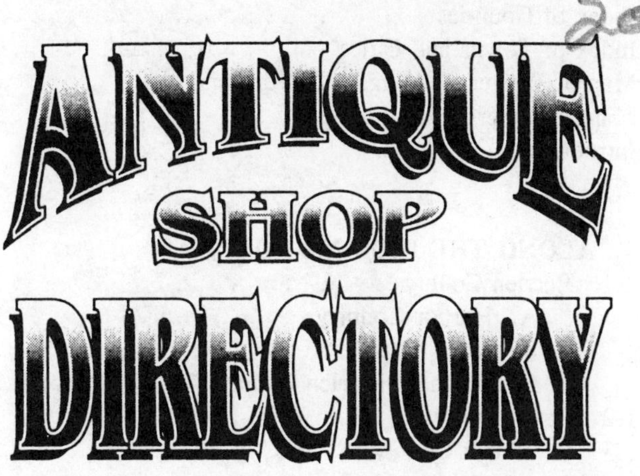

for Western Michigan

Listing All Known Shops and Malls
Days and Hours of Operation
Seasonal Changes in Hours
Telephone Numbers
Editor's Comments
Directions for Finding the Shops & Malls
Detailed Maps Showing Exact Locations
Recommended Points of Interest
Sources of Area Information
Index of Dealer Specialties
Calendar of Antique Shows

Publis
Edward Lawrence
Complete Antiqu Shop Directories
14906 Red Arrow
P.O. Box 297
Lakeside MI 49116
616 469-5995

TABLE OF CONTENTS

Index of Counties 4
Index of Towns and Cities 4
Map of Western Michigan, Lower Peninsula 7
Map of Upper Peninsula 8
Introduction 9

1. ALONG THE INDIANA BORDER:
1.1 Berrien County 11
A. Harbor Country 11
B. Niles Area 19
C. Northern Berrien County 22
1.2 Cass County 28
1.3 St. Joseph County 30
1.4 Branch County 34
1.5 Hillsdale County 37

2. THE I-94 ROUTE:
2.1 Van Buren County 43
2.2 Kalamazoo County 48
2.3 Calhoun County 54
2.4 Jackson County 60

3. SAUGATUCK TO LANSING:
3.1 Allegan County 66
3.2 Barry County 75
3.3 Eaton County 78
3.4 Ingham County 81

4. THE I-96 ROUTE:
4.1 Ottawa County 93
4.2 Kent County 97
4.3 Ionia County 105
4.4 Clinton County 110

5. THE M-46 ROUTE:
5.1 Muskegon County 113
5.2 Montcalm County 117
5.3 Gratiot County 121

6. THE M-20 ROUTE:
6.1 Oceana County 124
6.2 Newaygo County 127
6.3 Mecosta County 130
6.4 Isabella County 132

Table of Contents - continued

7. THE U.S. 10 ROUTE:
7.1 Mason County 135
7.2 Lake County 139
7.3 Osceola County 142
7.4 Clare County 143

8. THE M-55 ROUTE
8.1 Manistee County 145
8.2 Wexford County 147
8.3 Missaukee County 149
8.4 Roscommon County 150

9. THE M-72 ROUTE
9.1 Benzie County 153
9.2 Leelanau County 155
9.3 Grand Traverse County 159
9.4 Kalkaska County 164
9.5 Crawford County 165

10. THE U.S. 31 ROUTE:
10.1 Antrim County 166
10.2 Otsego County 170
10.3 Charlevoix County 171
10.4 Emmet County 175
10.5 Cheboygan County 183

11. THE UPPER PENINSULA:
11.01 Mackinac County 185
11.02 Chippewa County 187
11.03 Luce County 189
11.04 Schoolcraft County 191
11.05 Alger County 193
11.06 Delta County 194
11.07 Menominee County 197
11.08 Dickinson County 199
11.09 Marquette County 200
11.10 Iron County 203
11.11 Baraga County 205
11.12 Gogebic County 206
11.13 Ontonagon County 208
11.14 Houghton County 209
11.15 Keweenaw County 212

Selected Antique Shows 214
Index of Dealer Specialties 217

INDEX OF COUNTIES

(County, Tier & Sequence Number, and Page Number)

Alger County 11.05 193
Allegan County 3.1 66
Antrim County 10.1 166
Baraga County 11.11 205
Barry County 3.2 75
Benzie County 9.1 153
Berrien County 1.1 11
Branch County 1.4 34
Calhoun County 2.3 54
Cass County 1.2 28
Charlevoix County 10.3 .. 171
Cheboygan County 10.5 .. 183
Chippewa County 11.02 .. 187
Clare County 7.4 143
Clinton County 4.4 110
Crawford County 9.5 165
Delta County 11.06 194
Dickinson County 11.08 .. 199
Eaton County 3.3 78
Emmet County 10.4 175
Gogebic County 11.12 ... 206
Grand Traverse County 9.3 159
Gratiot County 5.3 121
Hillsdale County 1.5 37
Houghton County 11.14 .. 209
Ingham County 3.4 81
Ionia County 4.3 105
Iron County 11.10 203
Isabella County 6.4 132
Jackson County 2.4 60
Kalamazoo County 2.2 48
Kalkaska County 9.4 164
Kent County 4.2 97
Keweenaw County 11.15 .. 212
Lake County 7.2 139
Leelanau County 9.2 155
Luce County 11.03 189
Mackinac County 11.01 .. 185
Manistee County 8.1 145
Marquette County 11.09 .. 200
Mason County 7.1 135
Mecosta County 6.3 130
Menominee County 11.07 . 197
Missaukee County 8.3 ... 149
Montcalm County 5.2 117
Muskegon County 5.1 ... 113
Newaygo County 6.2 127
Oceana County 6.1 124
Ontonagon County 11.13 .. 208
Osceola County 7.3 142
Otsego County 10.2 170
Ottawa County 4.1 93
Roscommon County 8.4 .. 150
Schoolcraft County 11.04 . 191
St. Joseph County 1.3 30
Van Buren County 2.1 43
Wexford County 8.2 147

INDEX OF TOWNS AND CITIES

Afton 183
Alanson 180
Alden 167
Allegan 73
Allen 37
Allendale 96
Allouez 212
Alma 122
Amble 120
Athens 58
Bailey 116
Baldwin 139
Bangor 44
Baraga 205
Baroda 23
Barryton 131
Battle Creek 54
Bay Shore 175
Bear Lake 146
Belding 105
Bellaire 168
Benton Harbor 26
Benzonia 153
Berrien Springs 24
Bessemer 207
Blanchard 132
Blaney Park 191
Boyne City 174
Boyne Falls 174
Breckenridge 123
Bridgman 22
Brimley 188
Bronson 35
Brooklyn 65
Bruce Crossing 208
Brutus 180
Buchanan 21
Burlington 58

Index of Towns and Cities - continued

Cadillac 147
Calumet 211
Carp Lake 182
Carson City 118
Cassopolis 29
Cedar Springs 104
Cedarville 186
Champion 202
Charlevoix 171
Chase 140
Chassell 209
Cheboygan 184
Clare 143
Coldwater 35
Coloma 27
Colon 33
Concord 62
Constantine 31
Conway 177
Cooper Center 51
Coopersville 96
Copper Harbor 213
Cross Village 179
Crystal Falls 203
Dansville 88
De Tour Village 187
Decatur 45
DeWitt 110
Door 74
Doster 76
Douglas 67
Dowagiac 29
Eagle Harbor 212
East Grand Rapids 100
East Jordan 173
East Lansing 85
Eastport 169
Eaton Rapids 80
Eau Claire 24
Edwardsburg 28
Elk Rapids 166
Elsie 112
Elwell 122
Escanaba 195
Evart 142
Farwell 143
Fennville 69
Fouch (Traverse City) 155
Free Soil 138
Fremont 128
Gaastra 204
Galesburg 53
Galien 19
Ganges 67
Garden 194
Gaylord 170
Gladstone 195
Glenn 66
Gobles 47
Good Hart 179
Grand Haven 94
Grand Ledge 79
Grand Rapids 98
Grandville 98
Grant 127
Grass Lake 64
Grayling 165
Greenville 117
Gulliver 192
Hancock 211
Harbert 17
Harbor Springs 178
Harrison 144
Hart 125
Harvey 200
Hastings 77
Hickory Corners 75
Higgins Lake 151
Hillsdale 40
Holland 69
Holt 81
Homer 59
Honor 154
Houghton Lake 150
Houghton 210
Howard City 120
Indian River 184
Interlochen 160
Ionia 107
Iron Mountain 199
Iron River 204
Irons 141
Ironwood 207
Ithaca 121
Jackson 63
Jerome 41
Johannesburg 170
Jones 29
Jonesville 41
Kalamazoo 48
Kingsley 159
La Branche 198
Lake City 149
Lake Leelanau 156
Lake Linden 211
Lakeside 15
Lakeview 120
Lamont 96
Lansing 82
Lawrence 44

Index of Towns and Cities - continued

Lawton 45
Leland 157
Leonidius 33
Leslie 88
Levering 181
Lowell 102
Ludington 135
Luther 141
Mancelona 168
Manistee 145
Manistique 192
Manton 148
Marion 142
Marne 96
Marquette 201
Marshall 56
Mason 86
Mattawan 46
McMillan 190
Mears 125
Mecosta 130
Mendon 34
Menominee 198
Mesick 148
Middleville 76
Mt. Pleasant 133
Munising 193
Muskegon 113
Nashville 76
Negaunee 202
New Buffalo 11
Newberry 189
Niles 20
North Muskegon 115
Northport 157
Norton Shores 114
Oden 180
Okemos 85
Onekama 146
Orleans 106
Otsego 72
Ovid 111
Parchment 51
Paris 131
Parma 60
Paw Paw 47
Pellston 181
Pentwater 126
Petoskey 176
Plainwell 71
Portland 108
Potterville 78
Prudenville 151
Quincy 35
Ramsay 206
Rapid City 164
Reading 40
Remus 131
Richland 53
Rockford 103
Roscommon 152
Rothbury 125
Rudyard 188
Saranac 106
Saugatuck 68
Sault Ste. Marie 187
Sawyer 18
Schoolcraft 51
Scottville 138
Shelby 124
Shelbyville 74
Six Lakes 119
Sodus 26
Somerset Center 41
Somerset 42
South Haven 43
Sparta 104
Spring Lake 93
St. Johns 111
St. Joseph 25
St. Ignace 186
St. Louis 122
Stanton 118
Stanwood 130
Stevensville 23
Stockbridge 89
Sturgis 32
Sunfield 80
Suttons Bay 156
Tekonsha 59
Three Rivers 31
Three Oaks 13
Torch Lake 169
Traverse City 160
Turkeyville 57
Union City 36
Union Pier 14
Vestaburg 119
Vicksburg 52
Walhalla 138
Watervliet 26
Wayland 74
Webberville 92
Weidman 134
West Olive 95
Wheeler 123
White Piegon 30
White Cloud 129
Whitehall 116
Williamsburg 163
Williamston 89
Wyoming 98

Map of Western Michigan, Lower Peninsula

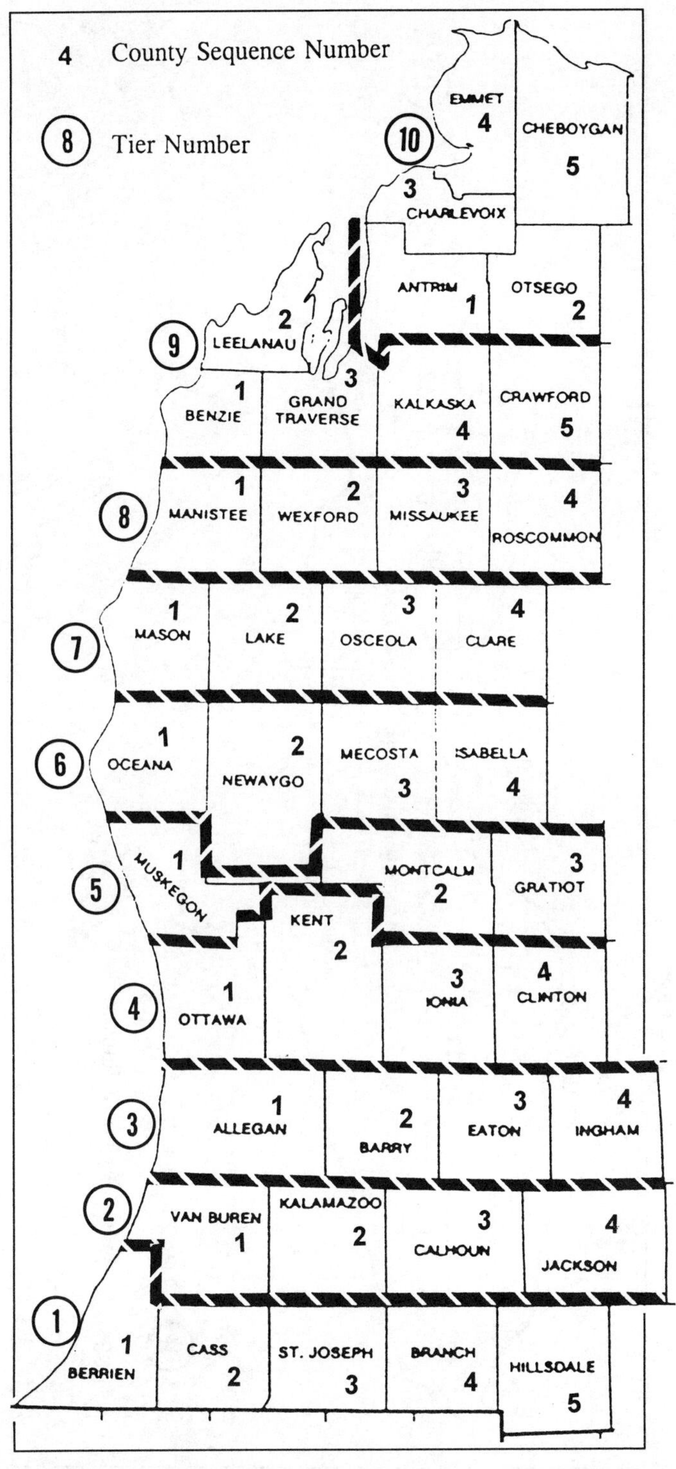

Map of The Upper Peninsula

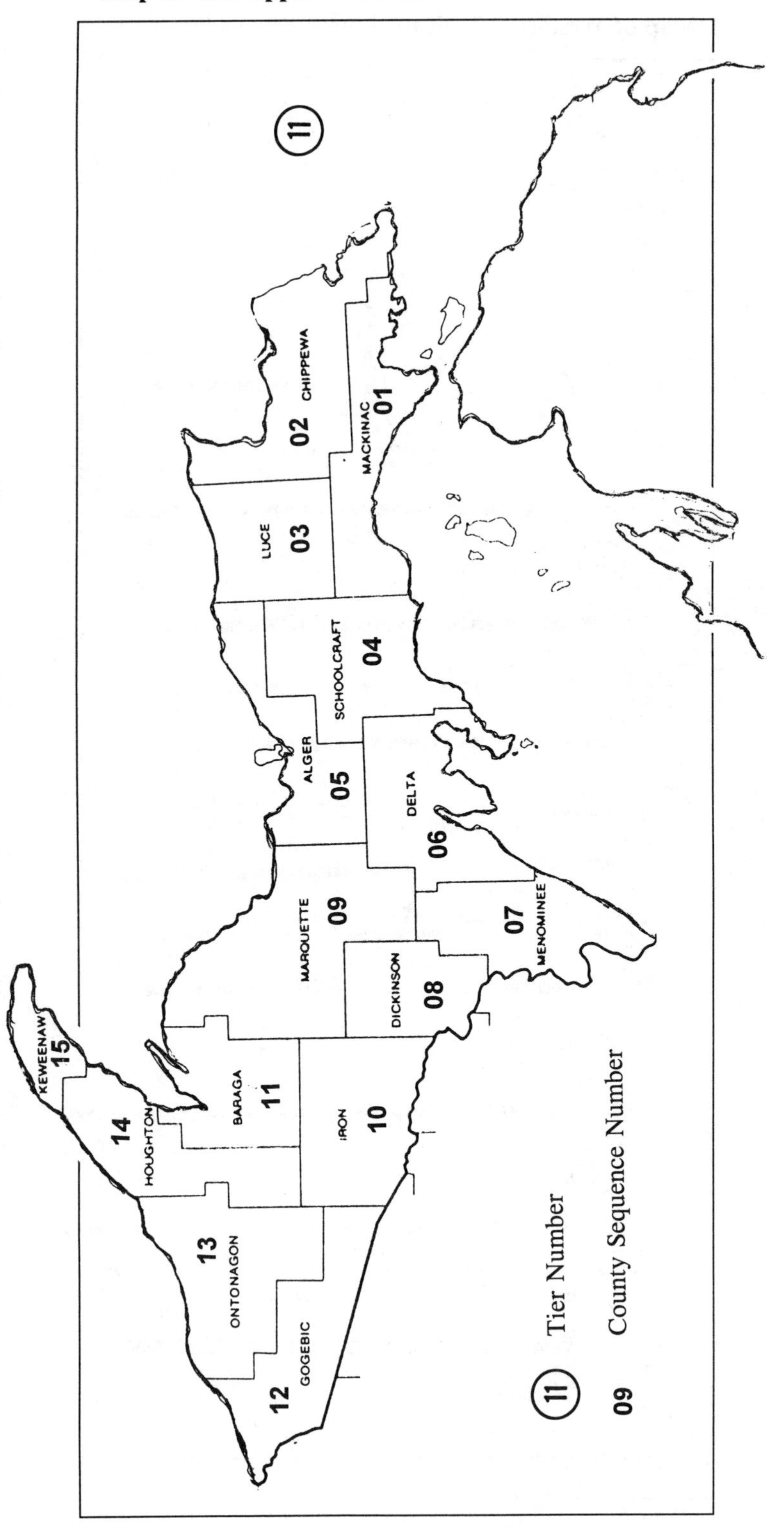

INTRODUCTION

This Antique Shop Directory is intended to provide the serious antiquer with a valuable tool for making his or her antiquing trips more efficient and enjoyable.

Information on Each Shop & Mall

Unlike some directories that list only those shops and malls that pay to advertise, this Directory lists ALL antique shops that could be identified. There is no charge to the antique dealer for the basic listing which contains the name of the shop or mall; the address; the telephone number; the days and hours of operation; seasonal variations; and a brief description of how to find the shop or mall. Dealers were invited to share the cost of printing this Directory, and provide readers more information, by placing a Display Ad.

Some shops and malls have a comment from the editor. Such comments were generally included for shops that have a specialty, and for shops that had a large number of gifts or reproductions.

Maps Showing Shop & Mall Locations

Another feature that makes this Directory unique is that the location of each shop and mall is shown on a map. These maps are indented only to show the general location of the shop, and should be used in conjunction with a more detailed street map.

Shops Not Included

Shops that were mostly gifts, crafts, used furniture, or reproductions were not included. Shops with gifts, crafts, used furniture, and reproductions were listed (and so noted in the editors comment) if they also had a significant number of antiques.

Order of Listings: By Tier By County

This Directory covers all the counties in Western Michigan and the Upper Peninsula, from the Indiana border on the south to Lake Superior on the north.

The listing of the shops and malls is organized as follows: the area has been divided into tiers of counties, each group consisting of a horizontal row of counties extending half-way across the state from Lake Michigan on the west to the center of the state (roughly the counties containing U.S. Highway 27).

The Upper Peninsula comprises the eleventh tier of counties. The tiers are numbered from south to north. Tier Number One is adjacent to the Indiana border; Tier Two lies just to the north, etc. Within each tier, counties are numbered from west to east.

Thus, each county can be identified with the number of the tier it is located in, and its sequence number within that tier. ***In this directory a county numbering system with a decimal point is used. The number to the left of the decimal point is the tier number, counting from the south; the number to the right of the decimal point is the county sequence number within that tier, counting from the west.***

Berrien County, at the southwest corner of the state, is in Tier One. Being the western-most county in that Tier, it has a county sequence number of one. Thus the identification number is 1.1. Eaton County is in the 3rd tier of counties north of the Indiana border, and is the 3rd county in from the west; thus it has an identification number of 3.3.

Caution

The editor traveled the entire area, visiting most of the shops or malls. Those not visited had the data verified by telephone. Efforts have been made to make this Directory as accurate and complete as possible. Antique shops do close and move, however, new ones open, and dealers may change their hours.

The editor cannot be responsible for any inconvenience due to erroneous or outdated information. Users of this Directory should also be aware that the hours given are "targets" of the dealers. Sometimes dealers go to auctions, estate sales, or away on personal business, and may not be there at a time when they are normally open. Also, some dealers do shows on certain weekends. Please take this into account, and be considerate if this occurs. Almost all shops and malls are closed Christmas, and some are closed other holidays. It is always best to call before driving out of your way to visit a shop.

Additional Information Provided

For the convenience of users of this directory, phone numbers of Chambers of Commerce are provided as a source of information about most counties. For many counties recommended points of information are indicated. Many of these recommendations are from the book: *Hunt's Highlights of Michigan*, by Mary and Don Hunt, published by Midwestern Guides.

TIER 1:
ALONG THE INDIANA BORDER

1.1 BERRIEN COUNTY

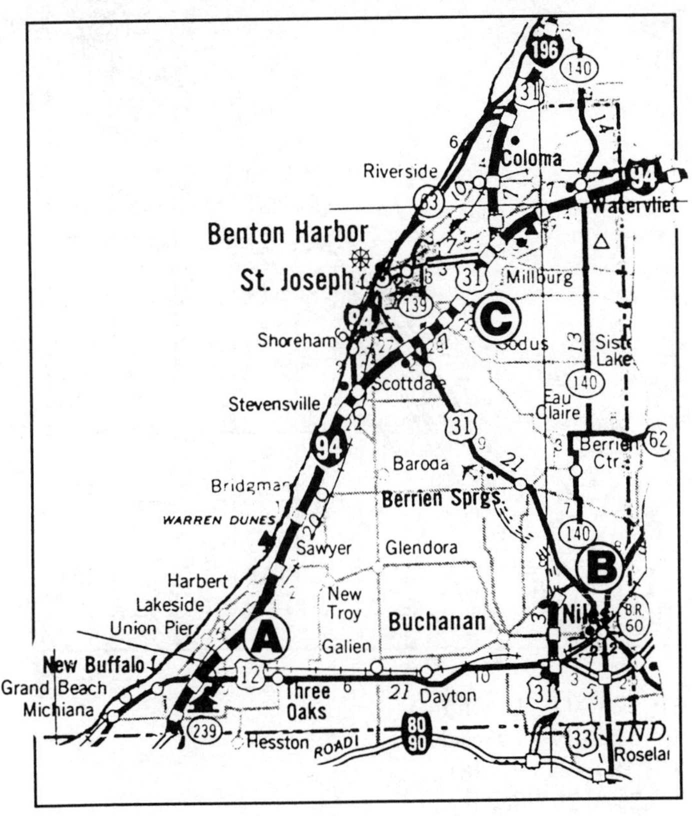

A. Harbor Country - See Detail Map
B. Niles Area - See Detail Map
C. Northern Berrien County - See Detail Map

A. HARBOR COUNTRY (Southwest Berrien County)

NEW BUFFALO

1 Country Corners
Southeast corner Wilson Road & U.S. 12
New Buffalo , MI 49117
No telephone listed. Open Sat. & Sun. 10 to 5
Midway between state line and New Buffalo.

1.1 a: Berrien County - Harbor Country - continued

HARBOR COUNTRY DETAIL MAP

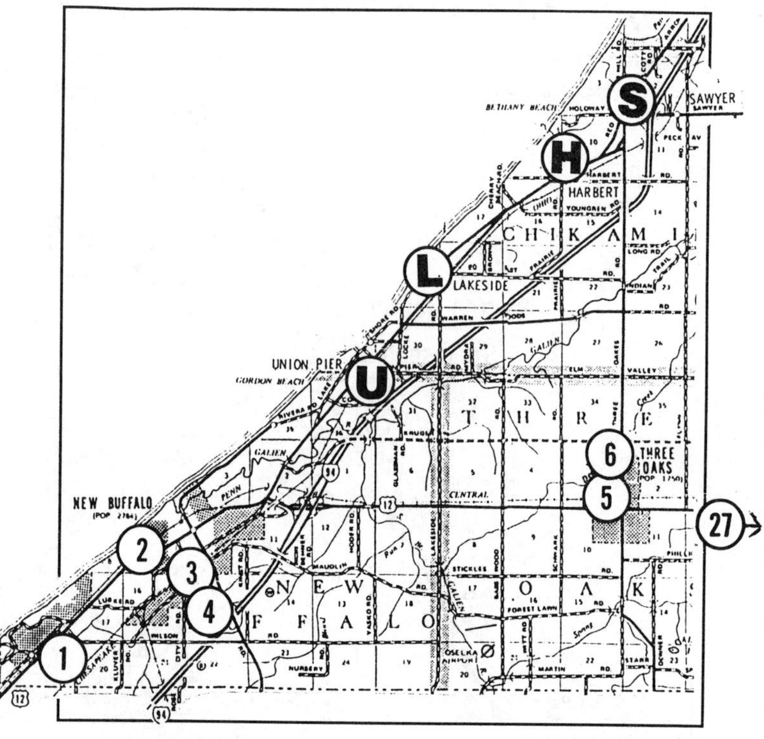

U: 7 to 11 - Union Pier
L: 12 to 17 - Lakeside
H: 18 to 23 - Harbert
S: 24 to 26 - Sawyer

Recommended Points of Interest:
* New Buffalo: Railroad Museum, 616 469-3166
* Three Oaks: Bicycle Museum, 616 756-3361
* See notice of the <u>Antique Trek</u> event on last page of this Directory. Held Veterans Day weekend each year.

For Additional Information:
* Harbor Country Chamber of Commerce, 800 362-7251

2 Memories
7 North Eagle, at the Red Arrow Highway
New Buffalo, MI 49117
616 469-0599
Daily 12 to 6, closed Wed.
West side of Red Arrow Highway, southwest of downtown.

3 The Roundhouse Antique and Craft Mall
530 S Whittaker St
New Buffalo , MI 49117
616 469-3166
Daily 11 to 6, closed Wed.
Several blocks toward New Buffalo from I-94 Exit 1.
100 dealers

4 Rainbow's End Antiques
18712 LaPorte Road (Whittaker Street)
New Buffalo , MI 49117
616 469-2655
May to Oct.: Daily 10 to 6;
Nov. to April: Sat. & Sun. 10 to 5
Southwest corner I-94 & LaPorte Road.
Established 1967.

THREE OAKS

5 Jenny's Antiques
9 N. Elm Street
Three Oaks, MI 49128
616 756-7219
Open by appointment only.
Downtown, west side of street.

6 Sentimental Journey Antiques
7 Chestnut Street
Three Oaks, MI 49128
616 756-3759
Sat. & Sun. 11 to 6; evenings by appointment.
North of downtown.

UNION PIER

7 The Plum Tree
16337 Red Arrow Highway
Union Pier, MI 49129
616 469-5980
Sat. & Sun. 11 to 6
East side of highway, south of the Union Pier light.
American, Irish and European pine, etc.

8 K.L.M. Galleries
16142 Red Arrow Highway
Union Pier, MI 49129
616 469-6957
Summer: Mon. to Sat. 10 to 5, Sun. 12 to 5;
Winter: Sat. 10 to 5, Sun. 12 to 5
West side of highway, just south of Union Pier Road.

9 Eagle Antique Mall
Red Arrow Highway
Union Pier, MI 49129
No telephone listed at press time. Sat. & Sun. 12 to 6
West side of highway, south of Union Pier Road.

10 Vintage Pine
15974 Red Arrow Highway
Union pier, MI 49129
616 469-6252
Sat. 12 to 6, Sun. 12 to 6 West side of road.

11 Antique Mall & Village
9300 Union Pier Rd
Union Pier , MI 49129
616 469-2555
Mon. to Fri. 10 to 5, Sat. 10 to 6, Sun. 12 to 6
I-94 Exit 6, southwest corner Union Pier Road & I-94
75 dealers, 10,000 square feet. Several buildings including main building, "church", Indian trading post, & diner.

LAKESIDE

12 Rabbit Run Antiques
15460 Red Arrow Highway
Lakeside , MI 49116
616 469-0468
Every day 10 to 6
West side of highway, north of Warren Woods Road.
English period pine, primitives, folk art, etc.

13 Plaza Antiques
14913 Lakeside Rd
Lakeside , MI 49116
616 469-2048
11 to 4 almost every day.
Lakeside Road north of Red Arrow Highway.

14 East Road Gallery
14906 Red Arrow Highway
Lakeside , MI 49116
616 469-5995 (or 616 469-1416 for appointment)
Sat. & Sun. 12 to 5; other times by chance.
West side of highway, just north of Lakeside Post Office.
Mission oak, Arts & Crafts Movement accessories. The owner of the East Road Gallery is the Publisher of this Directory. Stop in with suggestions for next year's edition.

15 Sally's Blue Cup Cafe
14866 Red Arrow Highway
Lakeside, MI 49116
616 469-6869
Summer: Daily 9 to 6 or so, closed Wed.;
Winter: Sat. & Sun. 9 to 6
West side of highway, next to Lakeside Antiques.
Nice tiny cafe with some pottery and other antiques for sale.

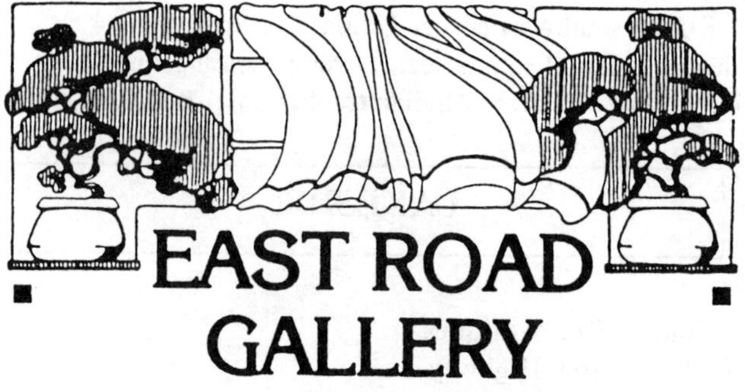

---

16 The Antique Complex
(formerly Harrison's Antiques)
14876 Red Arrow Highway
Lakeside , MI 49116
616 469-1158
Fri. to Mon. 11 to 6; Tues. & Thurs. by chance or appointment.

17 Lakeside Antiques
14866 Red Arrow Highway
Lakeside , MI 49116
616 469-4467 or 616 469-0341 for appointments
Summer: Sat. & Sun. 11 to 6, Mon. to Sat. 12 to 5, closed Wed.; Winter: Sat. & Sun. 11 to 6, Fri. & Mon. 12 to 5
West side of highway, north of East Road
2 recently enlarged red barn-like buildings.

HARBERT

18 Harbert Antique Mall
13889 Red Arrow Highway
Harbert, MI 49115
616 469-0977
Summer: Mon. to Thurs. 10 to 6, Fri. & Sat. 10 to 8, Sun. 11 to 6;
Winter: Thurs. & Mon. 10 to 6, Fri. & Sat. 10 to 8, Sun. 11 to 6
East side of highway.
24 dealers

19 Vintage Cargo
13887 Red Arrow Highway
Harbert, MI 49115
616 469-0977
Same hours as the connecting Harbert Antique Mall.
Home decorating showroom; fabric, reproductions, antiques
Moved from Lakeside in 1994

20 Global Dry Goods
Prairie Road & Red Arrow Highway
Harbert , MI 49115
616 469-5802 or 616 469-5273 for appointments
April to Oct.: Sat. & Sun. 11 to 6
Southwest corner Red Arrow Highway & Prairie Road.

21 Kalamazoo Antiques
13701 Red Arrow Highway
Harbert , MI 49115
616 489-5755
Sat. & Sun. 12 to 6
Northeast corner Prairie Road & Red Arrow Highway.
Art pottery, glassware, 50's decorative items, etc.

22 Judith Racht Gallery
13707 Prairie Road
Harbert , MI 49115
616 469-1080
Summer: Sat. & Sun. 10 to 5; Fri. & Mon. 12 to 5
Winter: Sat. & Sun. 10 to 5
Just east of Kalamazoo Antiques & the Red Arrow Highway
Art on the upper floor and antiques in the basement.

23 The Grand Bazaar
13581 Red Arrow Highway
Harbert , MI 49115
April to Dec.: Wed. to Sat. 10 to 5, Sun. 12 to 5;
Winter: By appointment.
East side of highway.
Large craft mall in front, antiques in back room.

SAWYER

24 Jeff's Trading Post
13212 Red Arrow Highway
Sawyer , MI 49125
616 426-3145
Summer: Every day 11 to 6; Winter: Every Day 11 to 5
West side of highway south of Sawyer Road
General line plus Hoosier Cabinets and glass & bottles.

25 Serendippity Antiques
Red Arrow Highway
Sawyer , MI 49125
616 473-2137
May to Sept.: Daily 1 to 5;
Oct. to April: Weekends 1 to 5:30
Southwest corner Red Arrow Highway & Sawyer Road.

26 Tara Hill Antique Mall
12816 Red Arrow Highway
Sawyer, MI 49125
616 426-8673
May to Sept.: Every day 11 to 5:30
October to April: Weekends 11 to 5:30
West side of Red Arrow Highway, North of Sawyer Road
and west of Three Oaks Road, next to the Book Rack.
Opened 1993

B. NILES AREA (Southeast Berrien County)

NILES AREA DETAIL MAP

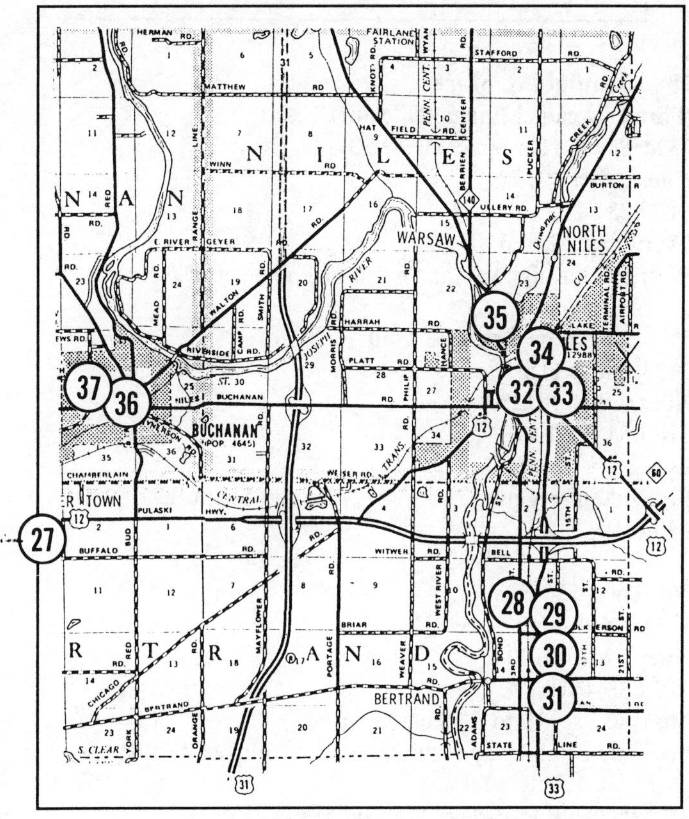

Recommended Points of Interest:

* Fernwood Botanical Gardens, Buchanan, 616 695-6491

* Fort St. Joseph Museum, Niles, 616 683-4702

For Additional Information:

* Four Flags Tourism Council, 616 683-3720

GALIEN

27 The Gray Barn Antiques, Collectibles, Junk

U.S. 12
Galien, MI
No telephone listed.
Fri. to Sun. 12 to 5
Southwest corner Pardee Road & U.S. 12.

NILES

28 Antiques & More
(Formerly called Junque N' Stuff)
2324 South 11th Street (U.S. 33)
Niles , MI 49120
616 683-4222
Every day 10 to 6
West side of highway,just north of Fulkerson Road.

29 Michiana Antique Mall
2423 South 11th Street (U.S. 33)
Niles , MI 49120
616 684-7001
Every day 10 to 6
East side of highway, between Niles and South Bend.
94 dealers.

30 Antiques Plus
2511 South 11th Street (U.S. 33)
Niles, MI 49120
616 683-4616
Mon. to Sat. 10 to 6, Sun. 11 to 5
East side of highway, 1 block south of Fulkerson Road.

31 Picker's Paradise Antique Mall
2809 South 11th Street (U.S. 33)
Niles , MI 49120
616 683-6644
Every day 10 to 6
East side of highway, between Niles and South Bend.
90 dealers, 35,000 square feet.

32 Four Flags Antique Mall
218 N. 2nd Street
Niles , MI 49120
616 683-6681
Memorial Day to Labor Day: Mon. to Sat. 10 to 6, Sun. 12 to 6;
Winter: Mon. to Fri. 10 to 5, Sat. 10 to 6, Sun. 12 to 6
Downtown, just north of the main street.
22,000 square feet, 60 dealers.

33 Yankee Heirloom
211 N. 2nd Street
Niles, MI 49120
616 684-0462
Mon. to Sat. 10:30 to 4:30, Sun. 12 to 4:30
Across from Four Flags Antique Mall

34 Sycamore Antiques & Collectibles
108 Sycamore Street
Niles , MI 49120
616 683-6652
Mon. to Sat. 10 to 5; Sun. 12 to 5
Around the corner from Four Flags Antique Mall.

35 Old Township Hall Antiques
1400 North Front Street (U.S. 31)
Niles, MI 49120
616 683-2960
Fri. to Sun. 10 to 5
West side of highway.

BUCHANAN

36 Millrace Antiques & Collectibles
122 East Front Street
Buchanan , MI 49107
616 695-2005; res.: 695-5257
Mon. to Sat. 10 to 6; Sun. 12 to 5
Downtown, south side of street.

37 Mollie Zelmer Antiques
118 West Front Street
Buchanan , MI 49107
616 695-1555
By appointment.
North side of street, one block west of downtown.
Glass, dolls, advertising, smalls.

C: NORTHERN BERRIEN COUNTY

NORTHERN BERRIEN COUNTY DETAIL MAP

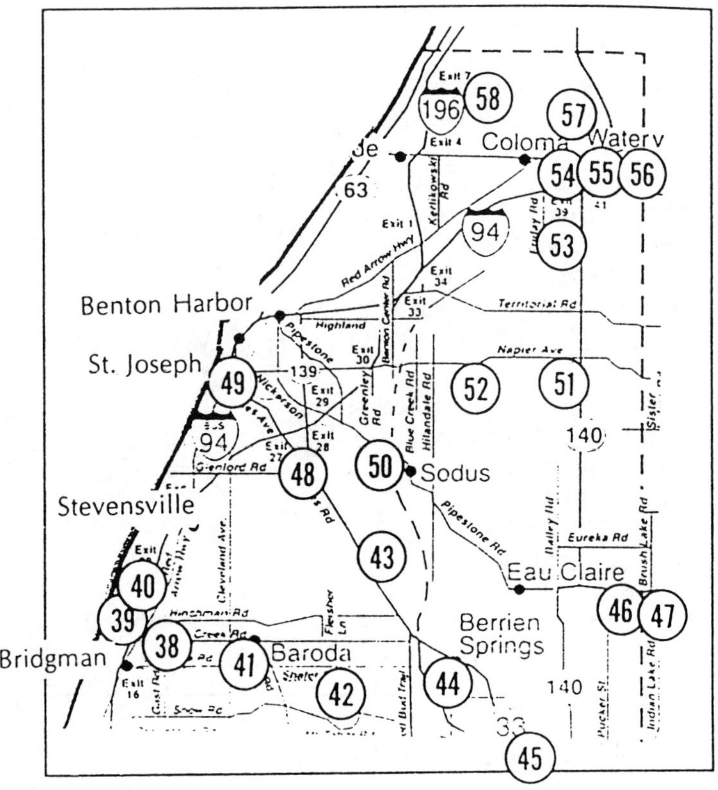

Recommended Points of Interest:
* Cook Energy Information Center, 616 465-6101
* Curious Kin's Museum, St. Joseph, 616 983-CKID

For Additional Information:
* Southwest Michigan Tourist Council, 616 925-6301
* St. Joseph Today, 616 923-6739

BRIDGMAN

38 Rideout Antiques
4369 Lake Street
Bridgman , MI 49106
616 465-6855
Mon. to Fri. 11 to 6 by chance or appointment. Closed last few weeks of tax season. (In front of CPA office.)
North side of street, west end of Downtown.

STEVENSVILLE

39 Bibliotiques Antiques
7622 Red Arrow Highway
Stevensville , MI 49127
616 465-5091
10 to 5 Every Day, (unless Mr. Westlake is at a show).
West side of highway, north of Cook Nuclear Power Plant.
Books, magazines, antiques.

40 Bill's Real Antiques
7566 Red Arrow Highway
Stevensville , MI 49127
616 465-3246
Noon to 6 Every Day
West side of highway, north of Cook Nuclear Power Plant.

BARODA

41 Classics
9004 First Street,
Baroda , MI 49101
616 422-1991
Summers: Mon. to Sat. 10 to 6; closed Jan. to April.
Downtown

42 Shawnee Road Antiques
638 East Shawnee Road
Baroda , MI 49101
616 422-1382
Summer: Every day 1 to 5;
Winter: Sat. & Sun. 1 to 5
Midway between Berrien Springs and Bridgman, south side of road.
Furniture, primitives, glassware.

BERRIEN SPRINGS

43 More & More Antiques & Collectibles
6659 U.S. 31 & 33
Berrien Springs , MI 49103
616 428-9084, 471-3030
Mon. to Fri. 9 to 5; Sun. 11 to 5
East side of U.S. 31 a block south of Rocky Weed Road.

44 Ole' Town Antiques Etc.
200 West Mars
Berrien Springs , MI 49103
616 471-3938
Summer: Sun. to Fri. 12 to 6;
Winter: Sun. to Fri. 10 to 6
Small shop just north of downtown, corner of U.S. 31.

45 Scherr's Antiques
11575 U.S. 31
Berrien Springs , MI 49103
616 683-9544
By chance Sat. & Sun. 12 to 5; closed Allegan show days.
3.5 miles south of Berrien Springs, east side of highway.

EAU CLAIRE

46 Oak Hill Antiques
6520 Brush Lake Road
Eau Claire , MI 49098
616 782-9292
March to Oct.: Wed., Fri., Sat. 9 to 5; Sun. 12 to 5;
Nov. to Feb.: By chance
Southwest corner Brush Lake Road & Eureka Road.

47 Walmar Antiques
55007 Brush Lake Road
Eau Claire , MI 49111
616 782-2315
Open most of the time by appointment or chance.
Corner of Brush Lake & Eureka Roads.

ST. JOSEPH

48 Anvil Antiques
3439 Hollywood Road
St. Joseph , MI 49085
616 429-5132
Mon. to Sat. 10 - 5:30; Sun. 12 - 5:30
East from I-94 Exit 27 on M-63 1 block, south on Hollywood one block.

49 Miller's Antiques & Collectibles
719 Gard Avenue
St. Joseph, MI 49085
616 983-2900
Mon. to Sat. 10 to 5, Sun. 12 to 5
From I-94 go north on Niles Avenue (M-63) past Hilltop Street; between Wendy's and Subway go west on Gard 1/2 block; north side of street.

SODUS

50 Virgo Antiques
3909 River Road
Sodus , MI 49126
616 927-3880
Sat. & Sun. 12 to 5; Closed Jan. 1 to May 1.
River Road & Naomi Street, south of Pipestone Road. From Exit 29 of I-94 go south on Pipestone Road, left at stop sign, right on River Road.

BENTON HARBOR

51 The Farm Antique Exchange
6400 East Napier
Benton Harbor, MI 49022
616 944-1500
Sat. & Sun. 11 to 5
3 miles east of I-94, south side of road.

52 Good Old Times Antiques
East Napier Avenue
Benton Harbor , MI 49022
616 925-8422
Sat. 11 to 5; Sun. 1 to 5; other times by chance or apt. apt.
1 mile east of I-94 Exit 30, south side of road.
Large selection of quality furniture and accessories.

WATERVLIET

53 Colonial Barn Antiques
580 North M-140
Watervliet , MI 49098
616 463-5838
Open April 1 to Dec.31
West side of highway, 3 miles south of I-94 Exit 41.

54 Annette's Antique Mall
340 North Main Street
Watervliet, MI 49098
616 463-3554
Mon. to Sat. 10 to 5, Sun. 11 to 4, closed Tues.
Downtown

55 Trade Winds Antiques
336 N. Main Street Downtown
Watervliet , MI 49098
616 463-8281
Every Day 10 to 5; Sun. 12 to 5
Collectibles, glass, postcards, and general line.

56 Historic House Antique Mall
349 N. Main
Watervliet , MI 49098
616 463-2888
Mon. to Sat. 10 to 5:30; Sun. 12 to 5
Downtown 28 dealers, 6,000 square feet.

57 Z's Antiques
7579 Red Arrow Highway West
Watervliet , MI 49098
616 463-5487
March to Dec.: Daily 11 to 4; Jan. & Feb.: by chance.
North side of road, mid-way between Coloma & Watervliet.

COLOMA

58 Millstone Antiques & Indian Relics
6162 Martin Road
Coloma , MI 49038
616 468-6667
May to Nov.: Fri. & Sat. 10 to 5
East from I-96 (Exit 7) on Hagar Shore 3/4 mile, south on Martin, first building on the west side.

1.2 CASS COUNTY

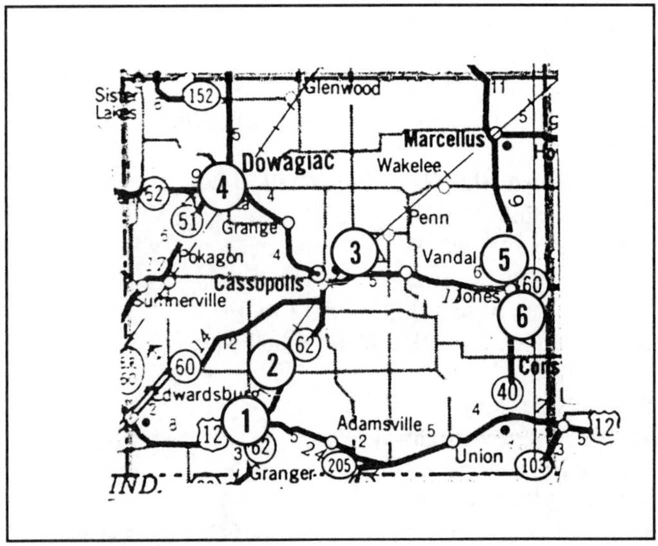

Recommended Points of Interest:
* Russ Forest Park & Newton House, 616 782-5652

For Additional Information:
* Dowagiac Chamber of Commerce, 616 782-8212

EDWARDSBURG

1 Argus Antiques
26878 W Main St (U.S. 12)
Edwardsburg , MI 49112
616 663-2883
Sat. to Wed. 12 to 5
West edge of town, north side of street.
Country primitives, military, jewelry, kitchen ware.

2 The Whistle Stop Antique Mall
66120 M-62 North
Edwardsburg , MI 49112
616 663-2659
Tues. to Sat. 10 to 6, Sun. 12 to 6
Two miles north of Edwardsburg on M-62 at Pine Lake Road.

CASSOPOLIS

3 Haymarket Shops
60405 Decatur Road
Cassopolis, MI 49031
No telephone listed.
Thurs. 12 to 3; Fri. 12 to 5; Sat. 10 to 5; Sun. 12 to 5
1 mile east of Cassopolis, 1/4 mile north of M-60, west side of road.
3 shops sharing large barn: Wildflower, C. Hebron, & Expressions in White.

DOWAGIAC

4 Olympia Books and Prints
208 South Front Street
Dowagiac , MI 49047
616 782-3443
Mon. to Fri. 10:30 to 4:30; Sat. 10 to 3
Downtown
Antiquarian books; prints.

JONES

5 Caroline's Antiques & Stuff
Main Street & Railroad Street
Jones, MI 49061
616 244-5997
Wed. to Fri. 10 to 4:30, Sat. 10 to 5, Sun. 12 to 5
Northwest corner Main & Railroad Street.

6 Hank's Antiques
61633 S. Main Street
Jones , MI 49061
616 244-5890
Wed., Thurs., & Sat. 10 to 5; Fri. 10 to 7
South of M-60, northeast corner Main & Railroad Street.

1.3 ST. JOSEPH COUNTY

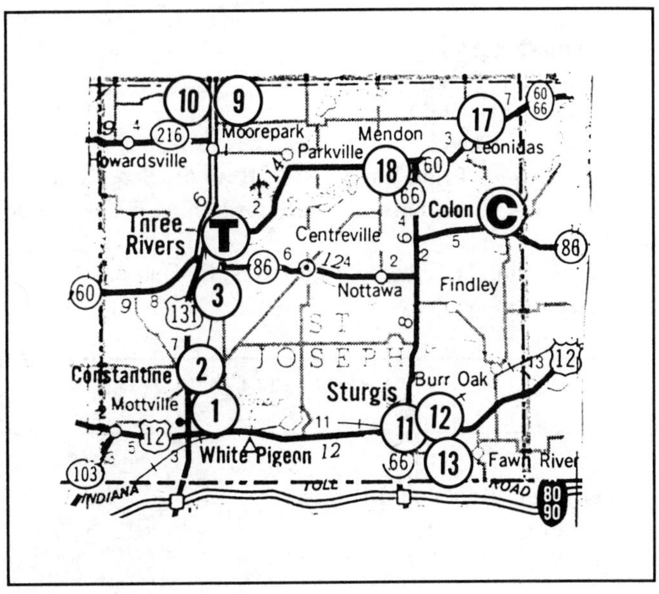

T: 4 to 8 - Downtown Three Rivers
C: 14 to 16 - Colon

Recommended Points of Interest:
* Colon Historical Museum, 616 432-3804

For Additional Information:
* Three Rivers Chamber of Commerce, 616 278-8193

WHITE PIGEON

1 Sweet Sensations Antiques
401 East Chicago Road (U.S. 12)
White Pigeon, MI
No telephone listed.
Northeast corner Glenwood Street & U.S. 12.

CONSTANTINE

2 Country Cupboard
145 South Washington
Constantine , MI 49042
616 435-2175
Mon. to Fri. 9 to 5:30; Sat. 9 to 3
Downtown, east side of street between Water & 2nd.
Flowers, gifts, and some antiques.

3 Antique Stoppe
63941 U.S. 131 North
Constantine , MI 49042
616 435-9445
Dec. to Sept.: Wed. to Sat. 11:30 to 5:30;
Oct. & Nov.: Fri. & Sat. 11:30 to 5:30
Two miles north of Constantine, east side of highway.

THREE RIVERS

4 Collectibles Unlimited
36 N. Main
Three Rivers , MI 49093
616 273-1596, 279-6377
Summer: Mon., Thurs. to Sat. 12:30 to 5;
Winter: Mon. to Sat. 11 to 5
Downtown
Dolls, bears, collectibles.

5 Antique Country Store
45 North Main Street Downtown
Three Rivers, MI 49093
616 273-1313
Wed. to Sat. 10 to 5, Sun. 12 to 5
Antiques, collectibles, crafts, gifts.

6 Main Street Marketplace
47 North Main Downtown
Three Rivers , MI 49093
616 279-2446
By chance or appointment.
Large shop; lots of furniture.

7 Antoinette's Antiques
51 North Main Street
Three Rivers , MI 49093
616 273-3333
Mon. to Sat. 10 to 5, Sun. 9 to 4
Downtown. Hunting, fishing, sporting antiques.

8 Olde Town Antiques
58 N. Main
Three Rivers , MI 49093
616 273-2596
Mon. to Sat 10 to 6, Sun. 11 to 5
Downtown, west side of street.

9 Links to the Past
52631 U.S. 131
Three Rivers , MI 49093
616 279-7310
Mon. to Sat. 10 to 6, Sun. 11 to 5, closed Wed.
North of Three Rivers, east side of highway.
Antiques, books, collectibles; 3,000 square feet.

10 Polish Peddler
52700 U.S. 131 North
Three Rivers , MI 49093
616 273-1412
Summer: Mon. to Sat. 12 to 5, closed Wed. & Sun.;
Winter: by chance.
Barn in back of the house; across from Links to the Past.

STURGIS

11 Gingerbread Emporium
109 East Chicago Road Downtown
Sturgis, MI 49091
616 651-1129
Wed. to Sat. 10 to 5 Gifts, crafts, antiques.

12 Antiques
1904 East Chicago
Sturgis , MI 49091
616 651-6455 Whenever home - ring bell.
East side of town at Vinewood, north side of street.
Garage on the side of the house.

13 Jan Douglas Antiques
30205 East Fawn River Road
Sturgis , MI 49091
616 651-7471
By chance.
4 miles southeast of town.

COLON

14 Woodcrafters
Elm & South Streets
Colon , MI 49040
616 432-3916
Memorial Day to Labor Day: Sat. 10 to 4
Two blocks south of downtown.

15 Village Posy Shoppe
210 E. State Street
Colon , MI 49040
616 432-2429
Tues. to Fri. 9:30 to 5:30; Sat. 9:30 to 1:30
Downtown
Gifts and antiques.

16 Memory Lane Antiques
107 E. State Street
Colon , MI 49040
616 432-3487
April to Oct. Mon., Thurs., & Fri. 10 to 4
All other days by chance or appointment.
Downtown

LEONIDIUS

17 Antiques
119 Depot St. at Route M-60
Leonidius , MI 49066
616 496-7928
Open by chance.
East end of town, south side of highway.
Antiques in the Rough.

MENDON

18 Emma's Emporium
137 West Main Street
Mendon, MI 49072
616 496-7250
Mon. to Sat. 11 to 6
Downtown, south side of street.
Gifts and some antiques.

1.4 BRANCH COUNTY

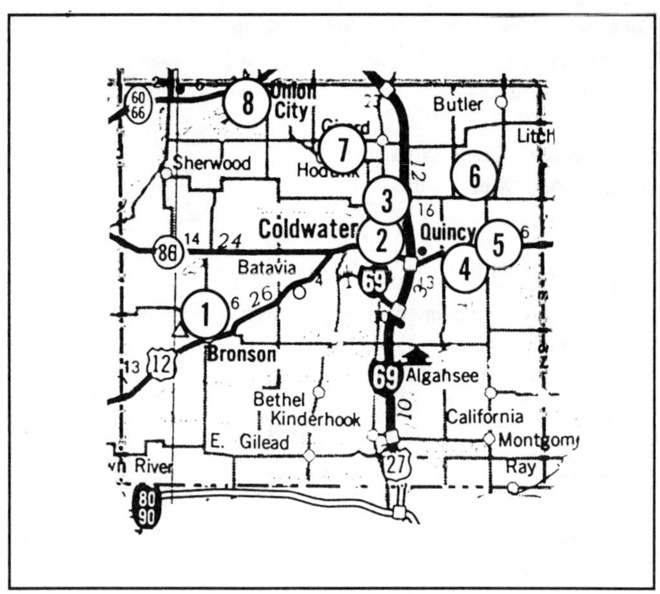

Recommended Points of Interest:
* Wing House Museum, Coldwater, 517-278-2871

For Additional Information:
* Branch County Chamber of Commerce, 517 278-5985

BRONSON

1 Shackleton's Antiques
103 East Chicago
Bronson , MI 49028
No telephone listed. Open by chance.
Downtown at stop light, corner Matteson & Chicago.

COLDWATER

2 Chicago Street Antique Mall
34-36 West Chicago
Coldwater , MI 49036
517 279-7555
Mon. to Sat. 10 to 5; Sun. 11 to 5
Downtown
19 dealers, 3 floors.

3 Fair Field Farm Antiques
868 Marshall Road (Old U.S. 27)
Coldwater , MI 49036
517 278-6485
Summer, by chance or appointment.
East side of road, 1 mile north of Coldwater.

QUINCY

4 Antiques, Collectibles, and Junque
929 West Chicago Road (U.S. 12)
Quincy, MI 49082
517 639-5803
Mon. to Sat. 9 to 4, Sun. 12 to 5
South side of highway at west city limits.

5 Collector's Paradise Antique Mall
47 East Chicago Road (U.S. 12)
Quincy, MI 49082
No telephone listed.
1 block east of light, south side of the street.
Parking is in the rear.

6 Terry Farwell
Rt. 3 Dayberg Road
Quincy , MI 49082
517 639-5010
By chance or appointment.
North from U.S. 12 on Quincy Grange to Dayberg, west on Dayberg, 3rd house on south side of road.
Paper, books, postcards, etc.

UNION CITY

7 Raymond's Country Barn Antiques
950 Union City Road
Union City , MI 49094
517 279-9370
Wed. & Thurs. 11 to 5 or by chance.
Mid-way between Union City and Coldwater, north side of road, just east of Burlington Road.
Primitives, postcards, jewelry.

8 A Plain Dealer
100 East High
Union City , MI 49094
517 741-3018
Open by appointment.
Downtown, south side of High Street, just west of Broadway.

An index of counties is found on page 4.

An index of towns and cities is found on pages 4 to 6.

An explination of the order in which counties are presented in this Directory is given in the Introduction on pages 8 and 9. (By Tier of county starting from the south, and within each Tier, counties are presented going from west to east.)

1.5 HILLSDALE COUNTY

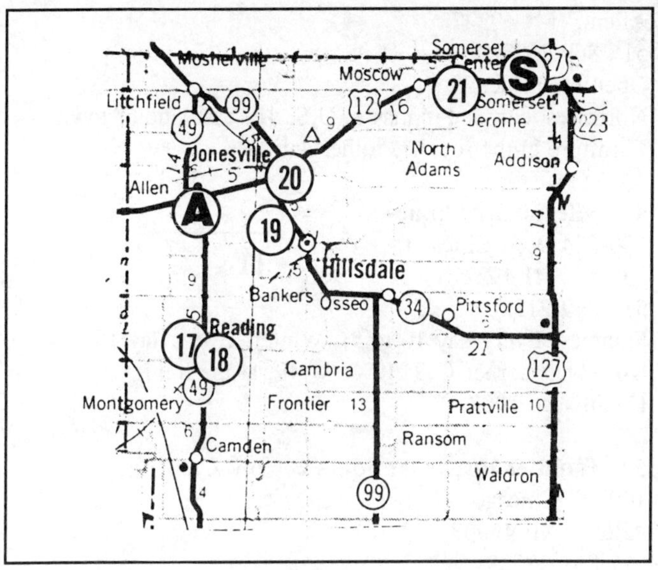

A: 1 to 16 - Allen
S: 22 to 25 - Somerset and Somerset Center

Recommended Points of Interest:
* Grosvenor House Museum, Jonesville, 517 849-9596

For Additional Information:
* Hillsdale Chamber of Commerce, 517 439-4341

ALLEN

1 Grandpa's Attic Antiques
222 East Chicago (U.S. 12)
Allen , MI 49227
517 523-2993
Thurs. to Tues. 10 to 5
East end of town.

2 1850's House Antiques, Collectibles, Crafts
113 East Chicago
Allen, MI 49227
No telephone listed. Hours not available.
Blue house, east end of town, south side of highway.

3 A Horse of Course
U.S. 12 & Prentiss
Allen , MI 49227
517 869-2527
Open by chance
Northwest corner Prentiss & U.S. 12, east side of town.
Furniture in the rough & other antiques.

4 Michiana Antiques
100-104 West Chicago
Allen , MI 49227
517 869-2132
Summer: Every day 10 to 5; Winter: Every day 10 to 4
Northwest corner U.S. 12 & M-49, at the light.
Established 1967.

5 Hand & Hearts Antiques & Folk Carvings
109 W. Chicago
Allen , MI 49068
517 869-2553
Summer: 12 to 5 every day except Wednesday;
Winter: Chance or appointment
Downtown, just west of light, south side of street.
Antiques and contemporary wood carvings.

6 Old Allen Township Hall Shops
114 West Chicago Road
Allen , MI 49227
517 869-2575
Every day 10 to 5
Downtown, north side of street.
12 dealers, 5,500 square feet.

7 Andy's Antiques
118 West Chicago Road
Allen , MI 49227
517 869-2182
Fri. to Wed. 10 to 5
Downtown, 4 doors west of light.

8 Timeless Treasures
West Chicago Road
Allen , MI 49227
517 869-2127
Sat. & Sun. 11 to 5; Mon. to Fri. by chance.
West of light, south side of U.S. 12.

9 J & Y Antiques
126 West Chicago Road
Allen , MI 49068
517 869-2289
Fri. to Sun. 10 to 6; Mon. to Thurs. by chance.
North side of street, west of light.

10 Diggers of Antiques
151 West Chicago Road
Allen , MI 49227
517 869-2319; 517 849-9715
Summer: Fri. to Tues. 11 to 5; Wed. & Thurs. by chance;
Winter: Fri. to Wed. 12 to 5
Downtown, a block west of the light, south side of highway.

11 160 W. Chicago Antiques
160 West Chicago Road
Allen , MI 49227
517 869-2492
Every day 11 to 6
Downtown, west of light.
Crowded with Victorian furniture, glassware, etc.

12 Peddlers Alley
162 West Chicago Road
Allen , MI 49227
517 869-2280
Summer: Every day 11 to 5; Winter: closed Wed.
West side of town, north side of U.S. 12

13 The Village Peddler
164 West Chicago Road
Allen , MI 49227
517 869-2280 shop
Summer: Every day 11 to 5; Winter: closed Wed.
West side of town, north side of U.S. 12.
Glassware, jewelry, some furniture.

14 Olde Chicago Pike Antique Mall
211 West Chicago Road
Allen , MI 49227
517 869-2719
Summer: Every day 11 to 6;
Winter: Every day except Tues. & Wed. 11 to 5.
West side of town, south side of U.S. 12.

15 Green Top Country Village Antique Mall
U.S. 12, 1/2 mile west of Allen
Allen , MI 49227
517 869-2100
Every day 10:30 to 5
1/2 mile west of Allen, south side of U.S. 12.
Complex of twenty historic structures; 65 dealers. One of the dealers specializes in Mission Oak.

16 Allen Antique Mall
9011 West Chicago Road (U.S. 12)
Allen , MI 49227
517 869-2788
Mon. to Sat. 10 to 5; Sun. 12 to 5
SWC U.S. 12 & Duck Lake Road, west end of town.

READING

17 Gallaway and Swafford
122 South Main Street
Reading, MI 49274
517 283-3603
April thru October: Thurs. & Fri. 12 to 5, Sat. 10 to 5
November thru March: Sat. 10 to 5

18 The Finer Things
112 East Michigan Street
Reading , MI 49274
517 283-2451
Wed. to Sat. 10 to 5
Downtown, across from post office, north side of street.
Glassware, clocks, pottery, furniture.

HILLSDALE

19 Carriage Anne Park Antique Mall
3390 Beck Road
Hillsdale, MI 49242
517 439-1815
Tues. to Sun. 10 to 6
West side of M-99, 3 miles south of U.S. 12 .
Opened 1994.

JONESVILLE

20 Antiques
Northwest Corner Evans and North Streets
Jonesville, MI 49250
Telephone number not available.
Hours not available.
1 block north of Town Hall, east end of downtown.

JEROME

21 Bundy Hill Truck Stop
9880 East Chicago Road (U.S. 12)
Jerome, MI 49269
517 688-4269
Summer: 24 hours Every Day;
Winter: 24 hours Fri. & Sat.; Sun. to Thurs. 6 a.m. to 10 p.m.
North side of highway.
Small collectibles & antique shop in back of the restaurant.

SOMERSET CENTER

22 Somerset House
12465 Chicago Road (U.S. 12)
Somerset Center, MI 49282
517 688-9816
May to Oct. : Thurs. Fri. Sun. & Mon.: 11 to 4:30; Sat. 9:30 to 6
South side of highway, 3 miles west of U.S. 127.

23 Bob's Antiques
12611 Chicago Road (U.S. 12)
Somerset Center , MI 49282
517 688-3596
March to December: Wed. to Fri. 11 to 5; Sat. 8 to 5;
South side of U.S. 12, 3 miles west of U.S. 127.

SOMERSET

24 Oak Hill Antiques
12500 Somerset Road (at 13940 U.S. 12)
Somerset, MI 49282
517 547-4195
Wed. to Sun. 10 to 6:30
Northwest corner U.S. 12 and Somerset Road, next to post office, one mile west of U.S. 127.
Opened 1994

25 Country Loft
14900 U.S. 12
Somerset, MI 49282
517 547-3313
Mon. to Sat. 10 to 6, Sun. 10 to 4
One quarter mile west of U.S. 127, south side of the highway.
Crafts and some antiques. Opened 1994.

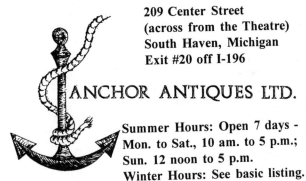

TIER 2
THE I-94 ROUTE

2.1 VAN BUREN COUNTY

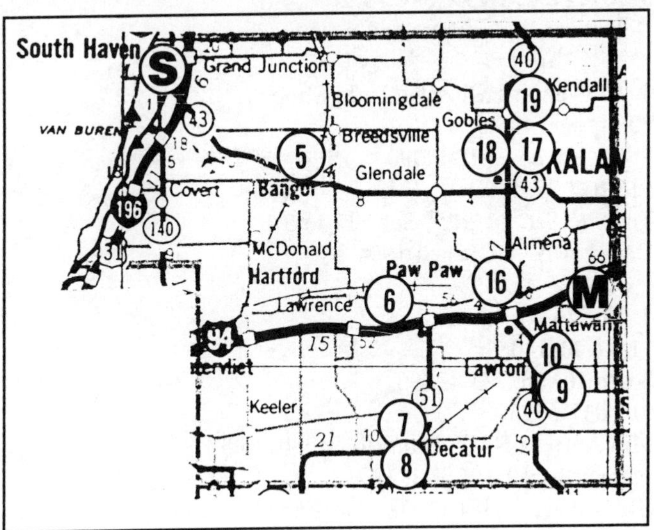

S: 1 to 4 - South Haven
M: 11 to 15 - Mattawan

Recommended Points of Interest:
* Lake Michigan Maritime Museum S. Haven 616 637-8078
* Liberty Bailey Museum, South Haven, 616 637-2351
* Kalamazoo Toy Train Factory, Bangor, 616 427-7927

For Additional Information:
* Lakeshore Visitors Bureau, 616 637-5252

SOUTH HAVEN

1 Anchor Antiques Ltd.
209 Center Street
South Haven , MI 49090
616 637-1500
May to Sept.: Mon. to Sat. 10 to 5, Sun. 12 to 5;
Oct.: Thurs. to Sat. 10 to 5, Sun. 12 to 5;
Dec., Feb. & Mar.: Fri. & Sat. 12 to 5;
April: Thurs. to Sat. 12 to 5; closed Jan.
Downtown, northeast corner Quaker & Center Streets.

2 Hidden Room Book Shop
518 Phoenix Street
South Haven, MI 49090
616 637-7222
May to Oct.: Every day 10 to 5
Downtown Antiques and used books.

3 Cheyenne's Closet Resale Shop
206 Center Street
South Haven, MI 49090
616 637-2955
Tues. to Sat. 11 to 5, Sun. 12 to 3
Downtown. Opened 1994

4. M-140 Antiques
11846 M-140
South Haven, MI 49090
616 637-6523
Mid-April to Nov.: Mon. to Sat. 10 to 5
Just north of I-196 Exit 18
(Paris Place at 321 Center and Ann & Shelley's at 548 Phoenix have crafts, gifts, and some antiques.)

BANGOR

5 Bangor Antique Mall
215 West Monroe
Bangor , MI 49013
616 427-8557
April to Dec.: Mon. to Sat. 10 to 5, Sun. 1 to 5;
Jan. to March: Fri. to Sun 10 to 5.
Downtown 3 Levels, 20,000 sq. ft.
(Earl's Coin & Jewelry nearby has some antique jewelry.)

LAWRENCE

6 L & R Antiques
50408 Red Arrow Highway
Lawrence , MI 49064
616 674-8562 Sat. & Sun. 10 to 5
1 mile east of Lawrence, north side of road.
Art glass, furniture and general line.

DECATUR

7 Golden Bell Antiques
211 N. Williams
Decatur , MI 49045
616 423-8197
June to Oct.: Thurs. to Sun. 10 to 5; other times by chance or appointment.
Large old mansion near downtown.

8 Antiques by Morence
201 East Delaware
Decatur , MI 49045
616 423-8607
April to Dec.: Every day except Wed. 10 to 6;
Dec. to Mar.: Fri. to Sun. 10 to 5
East of downtown in a residential area.

LAWTON

9 Lawton Antique Mall
131 S. Main
Lawton , MI 49065
616 624-6157
Mon. to Sat. 10 to 5; Sun. 12 to 5
South end of downtown, east side of street.
Parking lot between the two buildings.

10 Old Corner Drugstore & Ice Cream Parlor
156 North Main Street
Lawton , MI 49065
616 624-5261
Summer: Thurs., Fri., Sat. & Mon. 11 to 9; Sun. & Wed. 11 to 6;
Winter: Daily 11 to 6, closed Tues.
Downtown, southeast corner 2nd & Main
Small shop with ice cream parlor.
Glassware, lamps, furniture.

MATTAWAN

11 Tom Witte's Antiques
Front Street West
Mattawan , MI 49071
616 668-4161
By appointment.
One mile west of downtown, south side of road.
Antique tools.

12 William Lesterhouse Antiques
24020 Front Street
Mattawan , MI 49071
616 668-3229
Wed. to Sun. 12 to 5
Downtown

13 Halsey Dean Gallery
(Formerly Paul Millikan Antiques)
24028 Front Street
Mattawan , MI 49071
616 668-3510
Wed. to Sun. 12 to 5
Downtown
General line & Civil War items.

14 Red Hutch Antiques
(Formerly Front Street Antiques)
24030 Front Street
Mattawan , MI 49071
616 668-3023
Wed. to Sun. 12 to 5
Downtown

15 J's Antiques
24032 Front Street
Mattawan , MI 49071
616 668-3431
Wed. to Sun. 12 to 5
Downtown

PAW PAW

16 Paw Paw Antique Gallery
404 East Michigan Avenue
Paw Paw , MI 49079
616 657-5378
Mon. to Sat. 10 to 5, closed Wed.
East of downtown, south side of the street. Enter the parking lot from LaGrave Street, just west of the shop.
Located within a former church building.
6 dealers.

17 Back on the Farm
30609 M-40 Highway
Paw Paw , MI 49079
616 628-2400 (Res.: 616 628-5259)
May to Oct.: Wed. to Sat. 10 to 5:30; Sun. 12 to 5:30;
Nov. to mid-Dec.: Fri. & Sat. 10 to 5:30, Sun. 12 to 5:30;
Closed Mid-Dec. to April.
East side of the highway, 5 miles north of Paw Paw, just north of M-43.
Antiques, country crafts, gifts, dried flowers.

GOBLES

18 Country & More Antiques
21300 M-40
Gobles , MI 49055
616 628-4566
Sat. & Sun. 11 to 6;
Weekdays by chance or appointment.
West side of the highway, one mile south of Gobles.

19 Holmes Antiques
08757 M-40 North
Gobles , MI 49055
616 628-2035
Every day 11 to 6
East side of highway, two miles north of Gobles.
Furniture, collectibles, primitives.

2.2 KALAMAZOO COUNTY

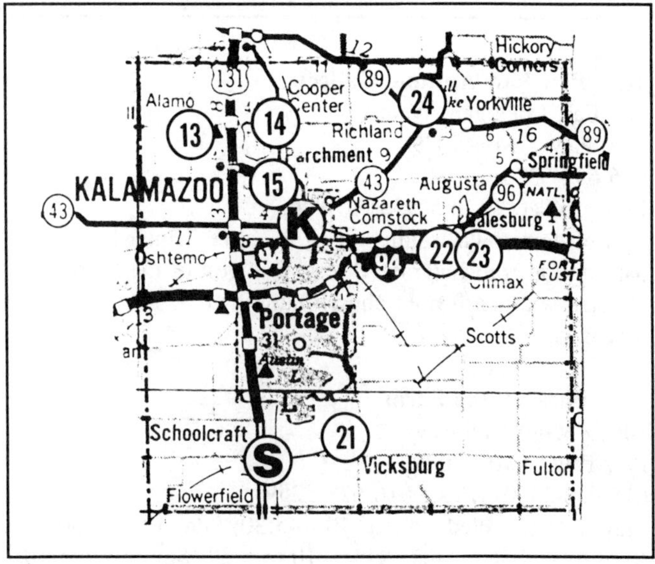

K: 1 to 12 - See Detail Map of Kalamazoo
S: 16 to 20 - Schoolcraft

Recommended Points of Interest:
* Public Museum, Kalamazoo, 315 S. Rose, 616 345-7092
* Kalamazoo Aviation History Museum, 616 382-6555

For Additional Information:
* Kalamazoo Visitors Bureau, 616 381-4003

KALAMAZOO

1 Souk Sampler
4614 West Main
Kalamazoo , MI 49007
616 342-9124 Mon. to Sat. 10 to 6
Westwood Plaza Shopping Center.
Men's and women's vintage clothing.

2 Gotta Have It Antiques
817 South Westnedge
Kalamazoo, MI 49008
616 342-8145 Daily 12 to 6
South of Vine Street. Art, antiques, decorative objects.

KALAMAZOO DETAIL MAP

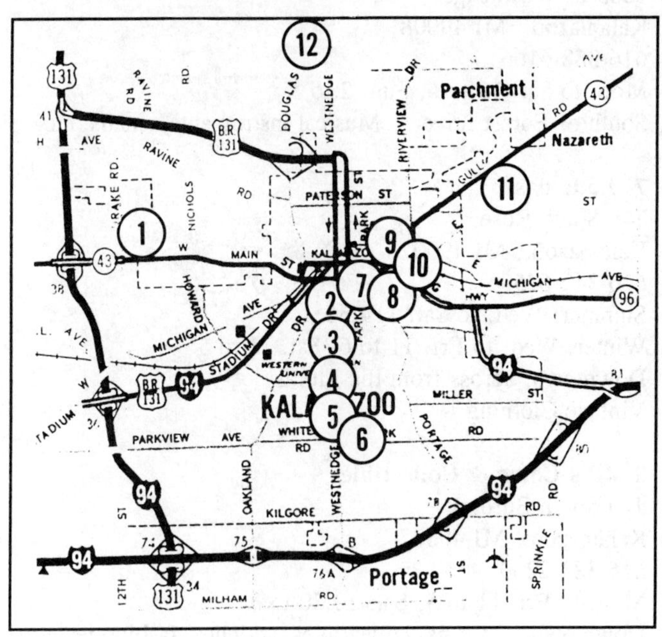

3 Aaron & Associates
824 S. Westnedge
Kalamazoo , MI 49008
616 342-8834
Mon. to Fri. 10:30 to 4:30, Sat. 9 to 12
West side of street near Vine Street.
Small shop; glassware, jewelry, etc.

4 Pennyrose
906 S. Westnedge
Kalamazoo, MI 49008
616 381-8747
Tues. to Sat. 12 to 6, Sun. & Mon. by chance.
West side of street, just south of Forest Street.
Antiques and art.

5 Attic Trash & Treasures
1301 S. Westnedge
Kalamazoo , MI 49008
616 344-2189
By chance or appointment.
Southeast corner Westnedge & Forest Streets.

6 Thieves Market
1305 S. Westnedge
Kalamazoo, MI 49008
616 388-6166
Mon. to Sat. 12 to 6, Sun. 2 to 5
South of Forest Street. Musical instruments, smalls, etc.

7 Lade das
346 South Rose
Kalamazoo, MI 49007
616 342-6759
Summer: Wed. to Sat. 11 to 5;
Winter: Wed. to Fri. 11 to 6, Sat. 11 to 5
Downtown, across from the Library.
Vintage Clothing

8 JP's Coins & Collectibles
420 South Burdick
Kalamazoo, MI 49007
616 383-2200
Mon. to Fri. 11 to 5, Sat. 10:30 to 3
Downtown Coins, collectibles, antiques, fashion jewelry.

9 The Emporium
313 E. Kalamazoo Ave.
Kalamazoo , MI 49007
616 381-0998
Mon. to Fri. 7 p.m. to 9 p.m., Sat. & Sun. 2 to 6
Downtown; northeast corner Kalamazoo & Pitcher.
11,000 square feet of furniture.

10 Heritage Architectural Salvage
402 East Kalamazoo
Kalamazoo , MI 49000
616 385-1004
Tue., Wed., Thurs. & Sat. 10 to 4
Downtown
Antique and reproduction architectural supplies.

11 Lola's Doll Shoppe
1930 Gull Road
Kalamazoo , MI 49007
616 344-2539 Weekdays 10 to 5, Sat. 10 to 2, closed Wed.
Southwest corner Gull & Colgrove, northeast side of city.
Small shop dealing in dolls.

12 Brook Farm General Market
3006 Douglas
Kalamazoo , MI 49004
616 342-6551
Tues. to Sat. 11:30 to 5:30
East side of road, a mile north of Business 131.

13 Alamo Depot Antique Mall
6187 West D Avenue
Kalamazoo , MI 49009
616 373-3886
Mon. to Thurs. & Sat.: 10 to 6; Fri. 10 to 8; Sun. 12 to 6
South side of road, 1/2 mile west of U.S. 131.
40 antique dealers, 120 craft dealers.

COOPER CENTER

14 Last Chance Antiques
8120 Douglas Avenue
Cooper Center (Kalamazoo) , MI 49004
616 381-5573
Thurs. to Sat. 11 to 5
East side of road between C and D Avenues.

PARCHMENT

15 Welborn Antiques
6300 N. Riverview
Parchment, MI 49004
616 345-3665 (Res.: 616 345-3665
Hours not available at press time.
North of Howlandsburg Road. Proposed to open late 1994.

SCHOOLCRAFT

16 The Fox Antique Co.
113 N. Grand (U.S. 131)
Schoolcraft , MI 49087
616 679-4018
Tues. to Sat. 10:30 to 5; Sun. 1 to 5

17 Ron's Grand St. Antiques & More; and Nettie Dee's
205 N. Grand
Schoolcraft , MI 49087
616 679-4774
Wed. to Sat. 10 to 5; Sun. 12 to 5
Downtown, west side of the street.
Two shops sharing the same space.

18 Schoolcraft Antique Mall
209 N. Grand
Schoolcraft , MI 49087
616 679-5282
Tues. to Sat. 10:30 to 5; Sun. 1 to 5
Downtown, west side of the street.

19 Norma's Antiques & Collectibles
231 N. Grand
Schoolcraft , MI 49087
616 679-4030
Mon. to Sat. 10:30 to 6; Sun. by chance.
Downtown, west side of the street.
Used furniture section on second floor.

20 Loving Ewe
245 North Grand
Schoolcraft , MI 49087
616 679-4205
Tue. to Sat. 10:30 to 5:30
North end of downtown, west side of street.
Gifts, accessories, some antiques.

VICKSBURG

21 Vicksburg Antiques, Gifts, & Crafts
107 S. Main Street
Vicksburg , MI 49097
616 649-2612
Mon. to Sat. 12 to 5, closed Wed. & Sun.
Downtown, just south of light.

GALESBURG

22 Antiques & Accents
37 West Battle Creek Street
Galesburg, MI 49053
616 665-4596
Tues. to Sat. 10 to 5, Sun. 12 to 5
Downtown, southwest corner Battle Creek & Mill Streets, next to Grant's Antique Market.
Opened 1993.

23 Grant's Antique Market
33 West Battle Creek Street
Galesburg , MI 49053
616 665-4300
Tues. to Sat.: 10 to 5; Sun.: 12 to 5
Downtown, southwest corner Battle Creek & Mill Streets.
From west on I-94 use Exit 85; from the east use Exit 88.
30 dealers, 8,000 square feet.

RICHLAND

24 Village Green Antiques
8023 Church Street
Richland , MI 49083
616 629-4268
By appointment only.
Southwest corner of Town Green in white house.

A calendar of selected antique shows in Western Michigan is given on pages 214 to 219.

An index of dealer specialties is given on pages 220 to 223.

2.3 CALHOUN COUNTY

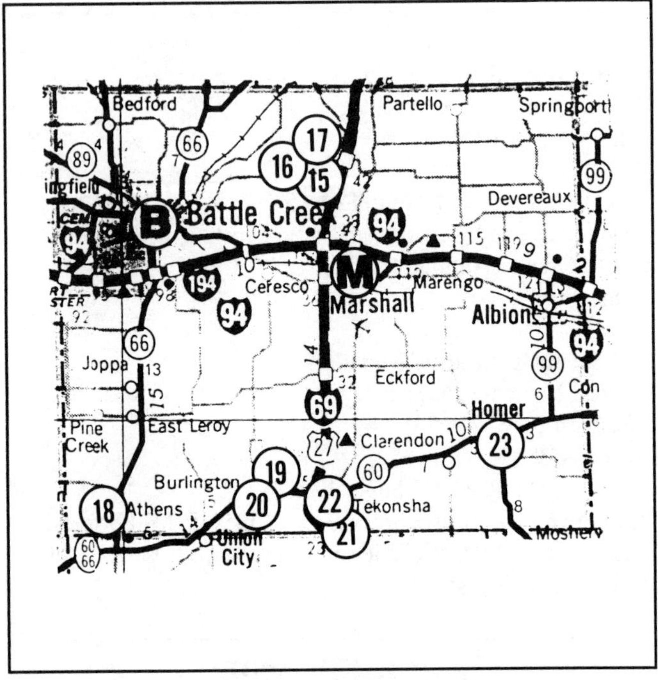

B: 1 to 3 - Battle Creek - see Detail Map
M: 4 to 14 - Marshall

Recommended Points of Interest:
* Kimball House Museum, Battle Creek, 616 962-2613
* Art Center of Battle Creek, 616 965-2613
* Kingman Museum of Natural History, 616 965-2613

For Additional Information:
* Calhoun County Visitors Bureau, 616 962-2240

BATTLE CREEK

1 Cherry Street Antiques
130 N. Division
Battle Creek , MI 49017
616 968-4155
By chance.
Southeast corner Cherry & Division several blocks northeast of downtown.

BATTLE CREEK DETAIL MAP

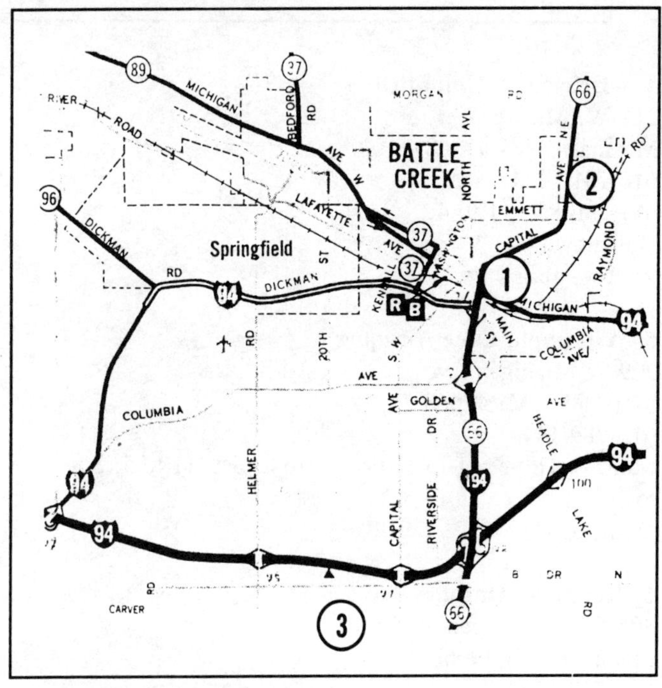

2 Battle Creek Upholstery

972 Capital
Battle Creek , MI 49017
616 963-6967
Summer: Mon. to Fri. 10 to 6;
Winter: Mon. to Fri. 11 to 2 and 3:30 to 6
Northeast of downtown at Capital & Montford Street.
Furniture & pottery in front of upholstery shop.

3 Karen's Keepsakes Gifts Old & New

11801 Sanoma Road
Battle Creek , MI 49015
616 979-2322
Opening Oct. 1994; call for hours.
I-94 Capital Avenue Exit, west on Beckley 1.5 miles to Sonoma, south on Sonoma 1.25 miles.
Barn in back of house.

MARSHALL

4 Heirlooms Unlimited
211 W. Michigan
Marshall , MI 49068
616 781-1234
Mon. to Sat. 11 to 4
Downtown
Pottery, glassware.

5 Pineapple Lane Antiques
209 W Michigan Ave
Marshall , MI 49068
616 789-1445
Mon. & Thrus. 11 to 5, Fri. 11 to 8, Sat. 11 to 5, Sun. 12 to 5
Downtown

6 Keystone Antiques
208 West Michigan
Marshall, MI 49068
616 789-1355.
Fri. 7 to 9 p.m.; Sat. 10 to 5; Sun. 1 to 5
Architectural and general antiques.

7 J & J Antiques and Tea Room
206 West Michigan Ave.
Marshall , MI 49068
616 781-5581
Mon. to Sat. 11 to 4 Tea room, gifts, antiques.

8 Little Toy Drum Antiques
135 W. Michigan Ave.
Marshall , MI 49068
616 781-9644
Mon. to Sat. 9:30 to 5:30
Downtown Gifts and antiques.

9 Baldwin Antiques
127 1/2 W. Michigan, lower level
Marshall , MI 49068
616 781-2678
Sat. 12 to 5:30 or by chance or appointment.
Downtown

10 Smithfield Banques
117 E. Michigan
Marshall , MI 49068
616 781-6969
Mon. to Sat. 10 to 5; Sun. 12 to 5

11 HilDor House Antiques
105 W. Michigan Avenue
Marshall , MI 49068
616 789-0009
Mon. to Sat. 10 to 5, Sun. 12 to 5
Downtown; good quality shop.

12 JH Cronin Antique Center
101 West Michigan
Marshall , MI 49068
616 789-0077
Mon. to Sat. 10 to 6, Fri. to 8; Sun. 12 to 5

13 Marshall House Antique Center
100 Exchange Street
Marshall , MI 49068
616 781-2112
Mon. to Sat. 10 to 5; Sun. 12 to 5
Just off the main street next to a little park, east edge of downtown, in a beautiful old mansion. 25 dealers.

14 Country House Antiques
19724 N. U.S. 27
Marshall , MI 49068
616 781-2046
Tues. to Sat.: 11 to 5; Sun. & Mon. by appointment.
6 miles north of Marshall, east side of road, north of N Dr.

TURKEYVILLE

15 The Olde Homestead Antique Mall
15445 N Drive North
Turkeyville (Marshall) , MI 49068
616 781-8119
April 1 to November 1: Tues., Wed., Thurs., Sat. & Holiday Mondays 11 to 5
NEC N Drive North & 15 1/2 Mile Road, 1/2 mile west of I-69 Exit 42.

16 Bushong's Antiques
18600 16 Mile Road
Turkeyville (Marshall) , MI 49068
616 781-5832
By chance or appointment.
Exit 42 of I-69, west 1/8 mile to 16 mile road, south on 16 mile road. Shop is in a stone house on east side of road.

17 Antique Barn
18935 15 1/2 Mile Road
Turkeyville (Marshall) , MI 49068
616 781-4293
Every Day 11 to 8
Southwest corner 15 1/2 Mile Road & N Drive North, 1/2 mile west of I-69 Exit 42.
Gifts, accessories, etc.

ATHENS

18 The Gryphon Antiques & Collectibles
131 S. Capitol
Athens , MI 49011
616 729-5500
Mon. to Wed. 10 to 5, Thurs. to Sat. 10 to 6
Downtown

BURLINGTON

19 Lincoln Inn Antiques
237 East Leroy (M-60)
Burlington , MI 49029
517 765-2170)
Mon. to Fri. 10:30 to 5, Sat. 11 to 5, Wed. & Sun. by chance or appointment.
North side of the highway.

20 Burlington Antiques & Collectables
114 Main Street
Burlington, MI 49029
517 765-2255
Summer: Wed. to Sun. 9 to 5
Downtown; Main Street is a block south of U.S. 12.

TEKONSHA

21 Kempton's Country Classics
1129 Marshall Road South (Old U.S. 27)
Tekonsha , MI 49092
517 279-8130
March to Dec.: Tues. to Sat. 10 to 5, Sun. & Mon. by chance;
Jan. to March: Sun. & Mon. by chance.
South of town, west side of road. Primitives, folk art, etc.

22 Bailey's Antiques
102 East Main Street
Tekonsha , MI 49092
517 767-4760
Fri. to Sun. 10 to 6
1 block east of M-60, northeast corner Main & Sophea.
Specializing in early pressed glass & Americana.

HOMER

23 Keepsakes Antiques & Collectables
125 W Leigh Street (M-60)
Homer , MI 49245
517 568-3629
Mon. to Sat. 10 to 5; Sun. 12 to 5
M-60 & M-99S, south side of highway.

2.4 JACKSON COUNTY

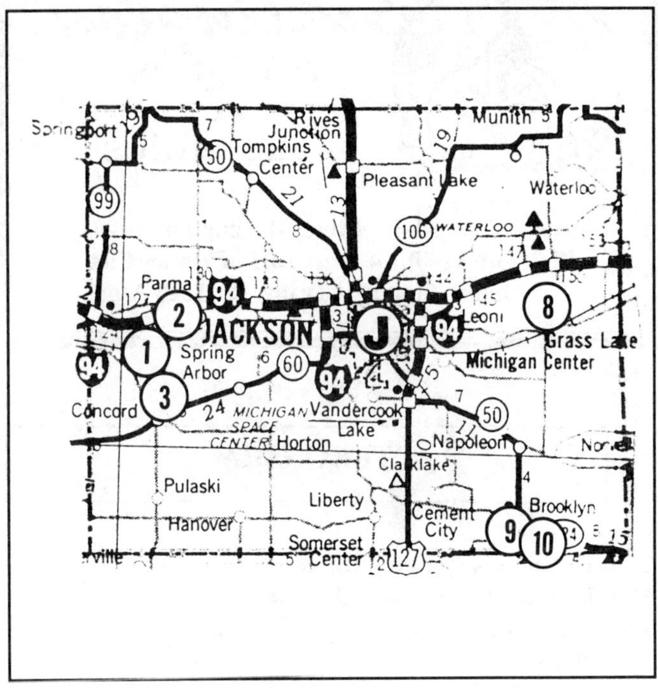

J: 4 to 7 - Jackson; see Detail Map

Recommended Points of Interest:
* Jackson Cascades, S. Brown St., 517 788-4320
* Ella Sharp Museum, Jackson, 517 787-2320
* Michigan Space Center, Jackson, 517 787-4425

For Additional Information:
* Jackson Visitors Bureau, 517 783-3330

PARMA

1 Harley's Antique Mall
13789 Donovan Road
Parma , MI 49224 (Mailing address: Albion)
517 531-5300
Every day except Christmas 10 to 6.
I -94 Exit 127, southwest corner.
12,000 square feet; opened 1992.

2 Cracker Hill Antique Mall
12000 Norton Road
Parma , MI 49269
517 531-4200
Mon. to Sat. 11 to 5; Sun. 12 to 5
Exit 128, north side of I-94. 26 dealers.

CONCORD

3 King Road Granary
12700 King Road
Concord, MI 49237
517 524-6006
April to Dec.: Wed. to Sun. 10 to 6
South from I-94 Exit 127 on West Concord Road 3.5 miles to King Road, west 1/2 mile; barn in back of house.

JACKSON

4 The Jackson Antique Mall
201 N Jackson St
Jackson , MI 49201
517 784-3333
Mon to Sat: 10 to 6; Sun. 12 to 6
Northeast corner Pearl & Jackson Streets, downtown.
40 dealers.

5 The Antique Shop
340 Otsego Street
Jackson, MI 49201
517 787-2033
Mon. to Fri. 8 to 5, Sat. 8 to 12
North side of Otsego just east of Washington, the one-way east-bound downtown loop street.
Western half of electric parts store.

6 Cash 'n Carry
817 E. Michigan
Jackson , MI 49203
517 782-3167
Mon. to Fri. 9 to 6; Sat. 9 to 5; Sun. 10 to 5
East of downtown, south side of street.
Mostly used furniture, but some antiques.

JACKSON DETAIL MAP

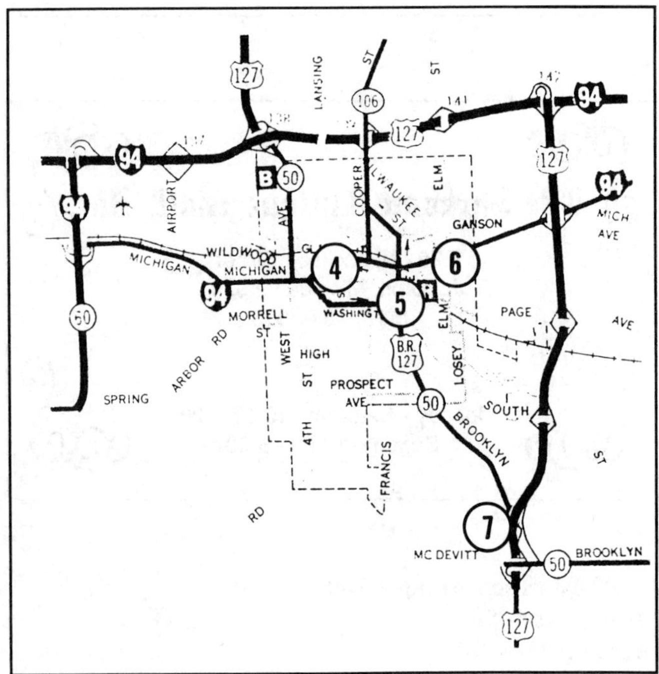

7 Browse & Bargain
1361 E McDevitt
Jackson , MI 49203
517 782-5101
Daily 9 to 6
Intersection of 127 & M-50.
Used furniture and antiques.

GRASS LAKE

8 Grand Illusion
103 & 201 East Michigan
Grass Lake , MI 48240
517 522-8715; 517 522-5822
Mon. to Sat. 9:30 to 4:30, Sun. 12 to 4
Downtown, south side of street.
Architectural salvage, art, jewelry.

BROOKLYN

9 Pinetree Centre Antique Mall
129 North Main Street
Brooklyn, MI 49230
517 592-3808
Mon. to Sat. 10 to 5, Sun. 12 to 5
Downtown, on the Square, east side of the street.
Opened 1994

10 Brooklyn Depot Antiques
207 Irwin Street
Brooklyn , MI 49230
517 592-6885
Summer: Fri. & Sat. 11 to 5, Sun. 12 to 4;
Winter: Sat. 11 to 5, Sun. 12 to 4; best to call for appointment.
A block east of M 50, south side of town.
Bells, office furniture, etc.

MAP OF ALLEGAN COUNTY

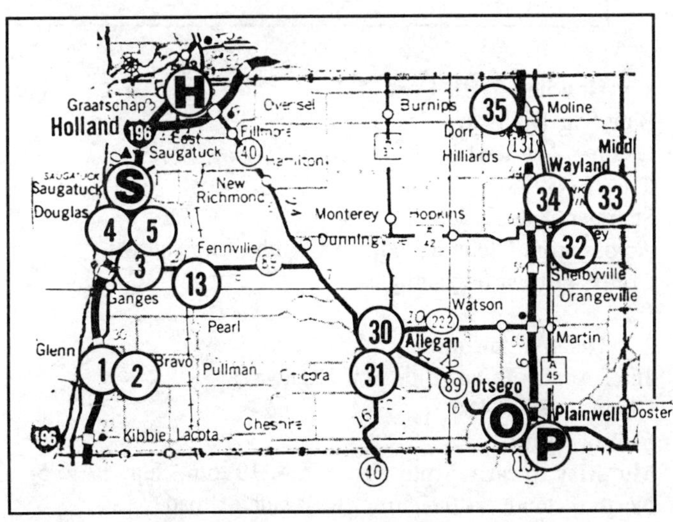

3.1 ALLEGAN COUNTY

(Map on preceding page.)

S: 6 to 12 - Saugatuck
H: 14 to 19 - Holland; see Detail Map
P: 20 to 23 - Plainwell
O: 24 to 29 - Otsego

Recommended Points of Interest:
* S.S. Keewantin Steamship Museum, Saugatuck, 616 857-2107
* 1886 Truss Bridge & Riverwalk, downtown Allegan
* Baker Furniture Museum, 147 Columbia Avenue, Holland, 616 392-8761
* Holland Historical Trust, 8 E. 12th, 616 392-9084

For Additional Information:
* Saugatuck Chamber of Commerce, 616 857-5801
* Allegan Chamber of Commerce, 616 673-2479

GLENN

1 Handled With Care
Blue Star Highway
Glenn , MI 49416
616 227-3908
Summer: Sat. & Sun. 11 to 4
Across from Glenn School, just south of downtown.
Crafts, gifts, a few antiques.

2 Helen's Antiques
1662 Adams Road (Blue Star Highway)
Glenn , MI 49416
616 227-3211
Mid-May to early Sept.: Fri. & Sat. 10 to 6, Sun. 12 to 6
North of town, at the curve, west side of road.

GANGES

3 Ekdahl's Antiques
2601 126th Avenue
Ganges , MI 49453
616 543-4477
April to Oct.: Every Day 9 to 5
Northeast corner Blue Star Highway & 126th Street.

DOUGLAS

4 Olde House Antiques
112 Center Street
Douglas , MI 49406
616 857-1623
Memorial Day to Labor Day: Thurs. to Sun. 11 to 5
Downtown
Historic 1872 house; Victorian furniture, & some new items.

5 Edwards Limited
36 Center Street
Douglas, MI 49406
616 857-1977
Memorial Day to Labor Day: Fri. & Sat. 10 to 7, Sun. to Thurs. 10 to 5:30;
April to Memorial Day: Daily 10 to 5:30;
Closed Jan. to Mar.
Downtown, east of Blue Star Highway.

SAUGATUCK

6 Handled With Care
403 Lake Street
Saugatuck , MI 49453
616 857-4688
Every Day 11 to 4
Lake & Allegan Streets, south of downtown.
Crafts, gifts, some antiques.

3.1 Allegan County - continued

7 Tafts Antiques
240 Butler
Saugatuck , MI 49453
616 857-2808
Downtown Small shop.

8 Country Store Antiques
120 Butler Street
Saugatuck , MI 49453
616 857-8601; if no answer call 616 396-1841
Summer: Mon. to Sat. 10:30 to 5:30;
Winter: By appointment.
Downtown
Open since 1953.

9 Centennial Antiques
3421 Holland Road
Saugatuck , MI 49453
616 857-2743
May to Oct.: Wed. to Sun. 12 to 5;
Oct. to May: Weekends only.
North end of town, east side of road.
Small shop; pottery, baskets, assorted country, etc.

10 Andy's Antiques
3400 block Blue Star Highway
Saugatuck , MI 49403
No telephone.
Summer: Mon. & Wed. to Sat. 10 to 5;
Winter: Thurs. & Sat. 10 to 5; closed Jan. & Feb.
West side of road at the Y intersection north of town.
Glass, pottery, smalls, furniture.

11 Jordan's Antique Mall & Indoor Flea Market
6413 Blue Star Highway
Saugatuck , MI 49453
616 857-4481.
Daily 11 to 5, closed Tues.
Highway A-2 just west of I-196, north end of town.

12 Fannies Antique Market
3604 64th Street
Saugatuck , MI 49453
616 857-2698 Open by chance.
North end of town, just north of Blue Star Highway.

FENNVILLE

13 Little Cedar Antiques & Accents
114 East Main Street
Fennville , MI 49408
616 561-2515
Mon. to Sat. 10 to 5; Sun. 11 to 5
Downtown, south side of street. Small antiques and gifts.

HOLLAND

14 Nob Hill Country Store Antique Mall
1261 Graafschap Rd.
Holland , MI 49423
616 392-1424
Mon. to Sat. 10 to 5:30
Two miles west and south of Tulip City Antique Mall.
West on Matt Urban Drive/48th St./146th St. to Graafschap Road, then south 1/2 block.

15 Tulip City Antique Mall
1145 S. Washington Ave.
Holland , MI 49423
616 396-8855
Mon. to Sat. 10 to 5:30; Sun. 12 to 5
Closed Easter, Thanksgiving, and Christmas.
East side of street. From southbound U.S. 31 take Exit 47B (Washington Avenue north).
12,000 square feet, 80 dealers.

HOLLAND DETAIL MAP

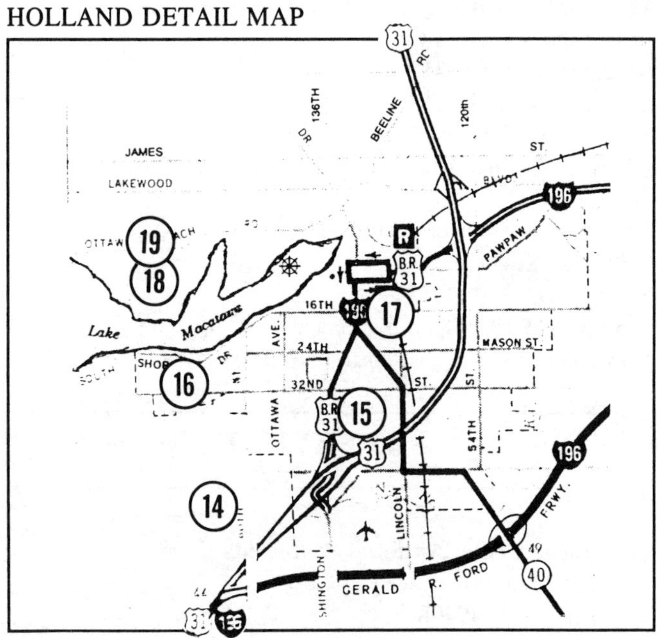

16 Stonegate Antique & Gifts
1504 South Shore Drive
Holland , MI 49423
616 335-3646
Memorial Day to Dec. 24: Mon. to Sat. 10:30 to 5:30, Sun. 12 to 5;
Christmas to Memorial Day: Tues. to Sat. 10:30 to 5:30, Sun. 12 to 5
1.5 miles west of downtown; west on 16th Street to South Shore Drive.

17 Antiques Etc.
383 Central Avenue
Holland , MI 49423
616 396-4045
Thurs. to Sat. afternoons.
Northeast corner Central & 16th Street

18 The Brick House
112 Waukazoo Dr.
Holland , MI 49423
616 399-9690
Summer: Every Day 10 to 5; Winter: Tue. to Sat. 10 to 5; Closed Dec. 25 to March 31.
Cross to north side of river, go west two miles on Douglas.

19 Janthrops of Holland
1200 Ottawa Beach Road
Holland , MI 49423
616 399-9691
Mon. to Sat. 10:30 to 5:30, Sun. 1 to 5:30;
May be closed in Jan.
Cross to north side of river, go west two miles on Douglas to 152nd Avenue.
Antiques, reproductions and home furnishings.

PLAINWELL

20 Plainwell Antiques
220 S. Main
Plainwell , MI 49080
616 685-9030
Wed. to Sat. 1 to 6
Just south of downtown, west side of the street.

21 Backdoor Antiques
220 South Main
Plainwell , MI 49080
No telephone listed.
Wed. 12 to 6; Thurs. to Sun. 12 to 5
Entrance on Grant Street, just around the corner from Plainwell Antiques.

22 Yesterday's Treasures
733 E. Bridge (M-89)
Plainwell , MI 49080
616 685-6693
Summer: Thurs. 12 to 7; Fri. & Sat. 12 to 5
7 blocks east of downtown, north side of street.
Small shop with primarily glassware.

23 Junk'n Stuff'n Things
633 E. Miller
Plainwell , MI 49080
616 685-5755
April to Dec.: Fri. to Sun. 10 to 5
East on M-89 to 8th, north on 8th to Miller, east on Miller.
Garage with antiques, collectibles, and used items.

OTSEGO

24 Harry J's & Missy
116 N. Farmer
Otsego , MI 49078 616 694-4318
Mon. to Fri. 10 to 5, Wed. to 6; Sat. 9 to 3
Downtown, east side of street just north of M-89.

25 Otsego Antiques Mall
114 W. Allegan St. (M-89) Downtown
Otsego , MI 49078
616 694-6440
Tues. to Sat. 10 to 6; Sun. 1 to 5

26 The Mercantile
506 W. M-89
Otsego , MI 49078
616 692-3630
Tues. to Sat. 10 to 5 Sun. 1 to 5
South side of M-89, west end of town.

27 Heritage Antique Mall
621 M-89 West
Otsego , MI 49078
616 694-4226
Tues. to Sat. 10 to 5, Sun. 1 to 5
106th Ave. & M-89, 5 miles west of Exit 49B of U.S. 131.

28 Lil' Red School House
793 West M-69
Otsego , MI 49078
616 694-2706; 616 694-9317
Sat. & Sun. 12 to 5, or by appointment.
2 miles west of Otsego, southeast corner M-69 & 108th Avenue.

29 Pine Hollow Farm
2020 108th Avenue
Otsego , MI 49078
616 694-9320
Sat. & Sun. 10 to 5
108th Avenue, east of M-89, down a long private road.

ALLEGAN

30 Water Street Place
420 Water Street
Allegan, MI 49010
616 673-5841
Mon. to Sat. 10 to 5, closed Thurs., open Fri. to 7; Sun. 12 to 5
Downtown

31 Dawn's Antique Barn
1259 Williams Bridge Road
Allegan , MI 49010
616 673-2253, 616 521-7529
Sat. & Sun. 10 to 5
South one mile on M-89 to Williams Bridge Street, south 6 blocks, east side of street.
Pottery, glass, flea market items.

SHELBYVILLE

32 Gun Lake Antiques
108 124th Avenue
Shelbyville , MI 49344
616 672-7902
By chance or appointment.
South side of 124th Street, just west of Patterson.

WAYLAND

33 The Hummingbird
2717 Patterson Road (Gun Lake)
Wayland, MI 49348
616 792-0778
Mon. to Thurs. & Sat.: 10 to 6; Fri. 10 to 8; Sun. 12 to 6.
6 miles east of US 131 Crafts & antiques.

34 Wayland Antiques & Gift Mall
142 S. Main Street
Wayland, MI 49348
616 792-0138
Mon. to Sat. 11 to 6, Sun. 12 to 4
One block south of light, west side of street.

DOOR

35 Back Door Antiques & Gifts
4219 18th Street
Door, MI 49323
616 681-9415
Mon. to Fri. 4:30 pm to 8; Sun. 1 to 8; Sat. by appointment.
Half block north of 142nd Avenue, east side of street.

3.2 BARRY COUNTY

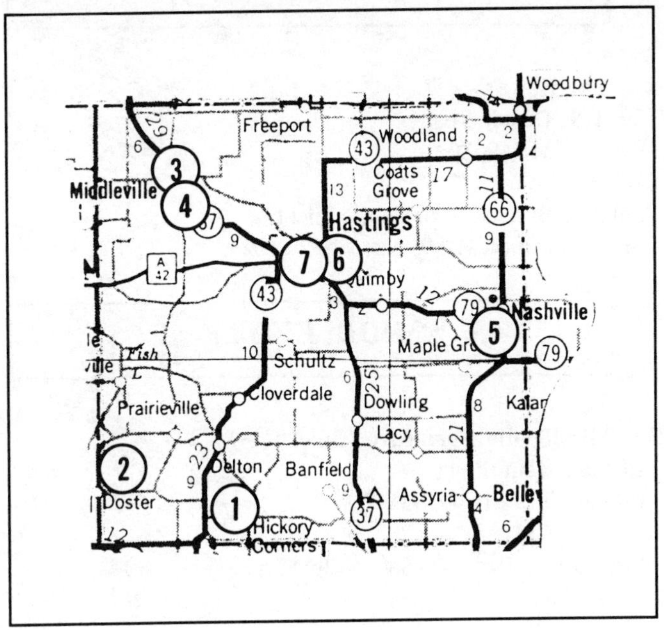

Recommended Points of Interest:
* Charlton Park Historic Village, Hastings, 616 945-3775
* Gilmore Classic Car Museum, Hickory Corners 616 671-5089

For Additional Information:
* Hastings Chamber of Commerce, 616 945-2454

HICKORY CORNERS

1 Hickory Hollow Antiques
14560 S Kellogg School Road
Hickory Corners , MI 49060
616 671-4222
Summer: Mon. & Tue. and Thurs. to Sat. 10 to 5; Sun. 12 to 5;
Winter: Sat. 10 to 5; Sun. 12 to 5
Southeast corner Kellogg School & Hickory Roads, 2 1/2 miles east of Gilmore Car Museum & M-43.
Furniture, collectibles, music and primitives.

DOSTER

2 The Elevator
12911 S. Doster Road
Doster , MI 49080
616 664-4676
Summer: By chance or appointment.
2 miles north of M-89, east side of road.

MIDDLEVILLE

3 Middleville Furniture Gallery
126 East Main Street
Middleville , MI 49333
616 795-3933
Mon. to Fri. 10 to 4; Sat. 10 to 12
Downtown

4 Mainstreet Middleville Antiques & Books
101 East Main
Middleville, MI 49333
616 795-8800
Tues. to Sat. 12 to 6, Sun. by chance
Downtown

NASHVILLE

5 Mar-Jay Collectibles
232 N. Main (M-66)
Nashville , MI 49073
616 945-5965
Thurs. to Sun. 10 to 4:30

HASTINGS

6 Hastings Antique Mall
142 East State Street
Hastings , MI 49058
616 948-9644
Tue. to Sat. 10 to 6, Sun. 12 to 5
Downtown, south side of the street.
Spinners & weavers gallery on 2nd floor.

7 Daval's Used Furniture & Antiques
2080 Gun Lake Road (M-37/M-43)
Hastings , MI 49058
616 948-2463
Summer: Sat. 9 to 5, Sun. 12 to 5, Mon. 9 to 5, Tues.- Fri. 9 to 8
1/8 mile west of Bob's Gun & Tackle Shop.
Glassware, cook books, reproduction oak furniture, etc.

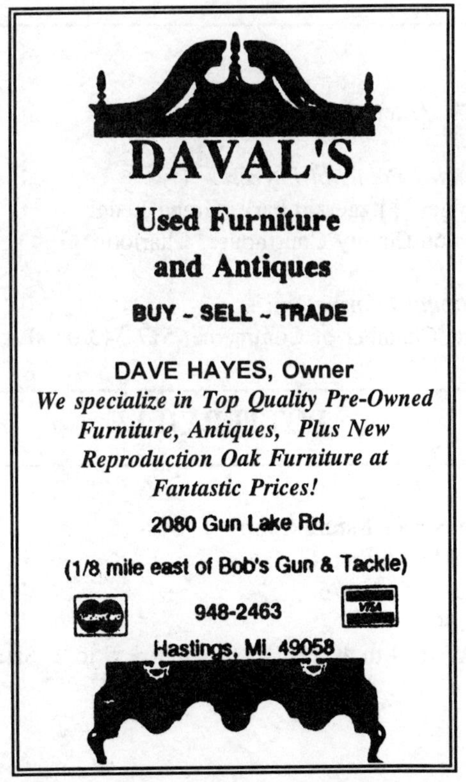

3.3 EATON COUNTY

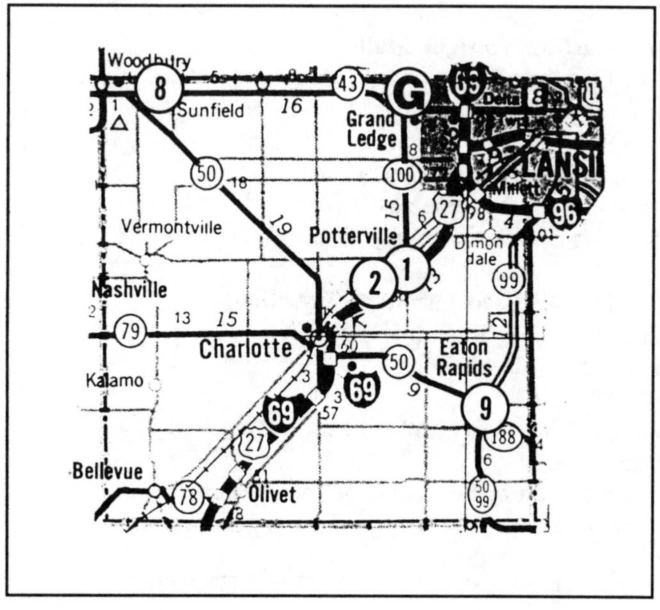

G: 3 to 7 - Grand Ledge

Recommended Points of Interest:
* The Ledges, Fitzgerald Park, Grand Ledge
* 1885 Eaton County Courthouse, Charlotte

For Additional Information:
* Charlotte Chamber of Commerce, 517 543-0400

POTTERVILLE

1 Main Street Estate Shop
202 West Main Street
Potterville , MI 48876
517 645-2909
Mon. to Wed. 9 to 4, Thurs. 2 to 7, Fri. 9 to 2, Sat. 1 to 5
Downtown

2 Bear Creek Trader
112 West Main
Potterville , MI 48876
517 645-7007
Mon. to Fri. 10 to 5, Sat. 1 to 5
Downtown, north side of street.
Western & Indian collectibles, some antique.

GRAND LEDGE

3 Best Wisches
312 S. Bridge Street
Grand Ledge, MI 48837
517 622-1524
Mon. to Sat. 10 to 5:30, Sun. by chance
Downtown
Antiques & collectibles; some 40's & 50's odds & ends.

4 Bridge View Consignment Boutique
202 South Bridge Street
Grand Ledge, MI 48837
517 627-0830
Wed. to Sat. 10 to 6, Sun. 12 to 5
Downtown

5 Fifties & Such
201 S. Bridge Street
Grand Ledge, MI 48837
517 627-3771
Tues. to Sat. 10 to 8, Sun. 12 to 6
Downtown, through the Bridge View Consignment Boutique.
Soda fountain & collectibles shop.

6 Bridge Street Church Antiques Mall
200 N. Bridge Street
Grand Ledge , MI 48837
517 627-8637
Wed. to Sat. 10 to 5; Sun. 12 to 5
Downtown, just north of the river.
2 floors.

7 Timeless Treasures
215 N. Bridge Street
Grand Ledge, MI 48837
517 627-7476
Tues. 1 to 6, Wed. to Fri. 9:30 to 5, Sat. 9 to 7
Downtown

SUNFIELD

8 J n M's Just Nostalgia Memories
12821 Sunfield Highway
Sunfield, MI 48890
517 566-7227
Wed. to Sat. 12 to 5
West side of street, south of M-43, behind the Marathon Station.
Glassware, etc.

EATON RAPIDS

9 Miller's Crossing Art & Antiques
203 South Main Street
Eaton Rapids, MI 48827
517 663-6668
Summer: Mon. to Sat. 10 to 5, Sun. 12 to 5;
Winter: Mon. to Fri. 10 to 5
Downtown, west side of street, across from City Hall.
Mall opened 1993.

3.4 INGHAM COUNTY

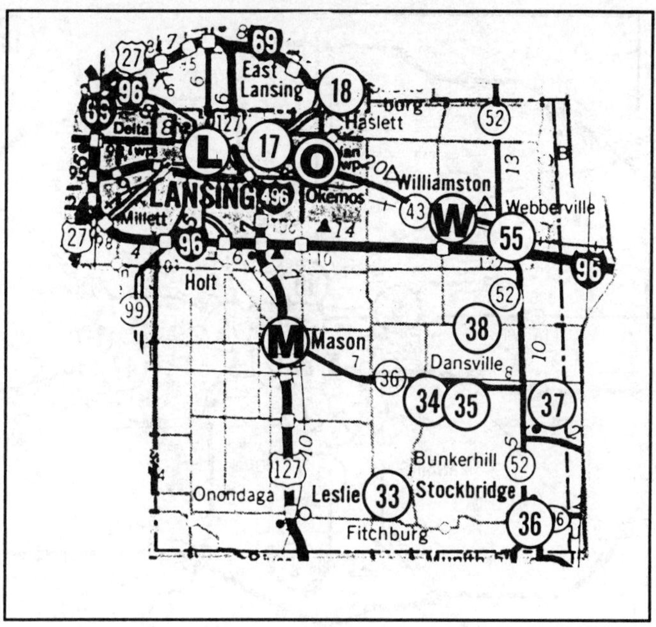

L: 1 to 16 - Lansing, see Detail Map
O: 19 to 22 - Okemos
M: 23 to 32 - Mason
W: 39 to 54 - Williamston

Recommended Points of Interest:
* Beal Gardens, East Lansing, 517 355-9582
* Kresge Art Museum, East Lansing, 517 355-7631
* Ingham County Courthouse, Mason

For Additional Information:
* Mason Chamber of Commerce, 517 676-1046

HOLT

1 Antiques Plus
Cedar Park Shopping Center
2495 N. Cedar
Holt , MI 48842
517 694-5767
Mon. to Fri. 11 to 6, Sat. 10 to 5, Sun. 12 to 5, Thurs. to 9
West side of highway, just south of I-96.

3.4 Ingham County - continued

LANSING DETAIL MAP

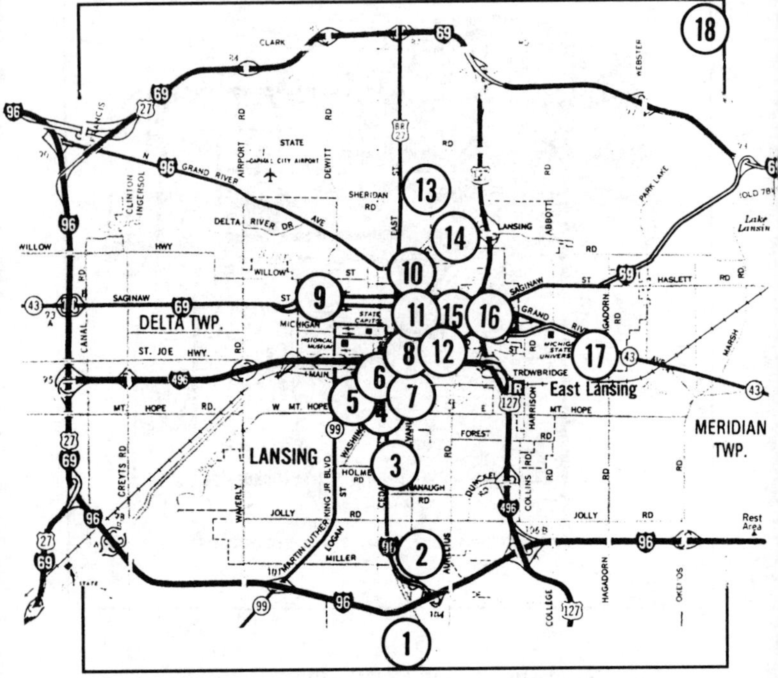

Recommended Points of Interest:
* State Capitol, 517 335-1483
* Michigan Historical Museum, 517 373-2559
* City Market, Cedar & Shiawassee
* Turner Dodge House, 517 483-4220

For Additional Information:
* Lansing Visitors Bureau, 517 487-6800

LANSING

2 Antique Connection
5411 South Cedar St.
Lansing , MI 48911
517 882-8700
Mon. to Fri. 10 to 9; Sat. 10 to 6; Sun. 12 to 5
East side of street, in back of Furniture Connection, 1 mile north of I-96, 1 block south of Jolly Road.
Crafts, glass, smalls, with some antique furniture used as accents in the furniture store. 90 antique & crafts booths.

3 St. Luke's Antiques
3016 South Cedar
Lansing, MI
517 882-5364
Sat. 1 to 5, Sun. 1 to 4:30
West side of street.

4 Stark Raving Neon
1147 South Washington
Lansing , MI 48910
517 487-1310
By chance or appointment.
East side of the street.
Neon signs and art.

5 River Point Emporium
1136 South Washington
Lansing, MI 48910
517 487-8778
Mon. to Fri. 11:45 to 6, Sat. 10:30 to 5
West side of street.

6 Somebody Else's Stuff
1137 South Washington
Lansing, MI 48910
517 482-8886
Mon. to Fri. 11 to 6; Sat. 12 to 5
East side of the street.

7 Gallimores
1113 South Washington
Lansing, MI 48910
517 485-9843
Wed. to Sat. 11 to 5
East side of street.
Opened 1994.
Antiques, collectibles, and reproductions.

8 Rebecca's Antiques
1101 South Washington
Lansing , MI 48910
517 485-6076
Mon. to Sat. 11 to 5
Southeast corner Washington & Elm Streets.

9 Bohnet's
1712 W. Saginaw Street
Lansing , MI 48915
517 482-2654
Mon. to Fri. 8 to 5; also Sat. in winter.
East-bound M-43, west of downtown.
Light fixtures.

10 Old Town Merchandise Mart
319 East Grand River
Lansing, MI
517 485-8335
A quarter block west of Center Street, north side of street.
Used furniture, some antiques.

11 Triola's
119 Pere Marquette
Lansing , MI 48912
517 484-5414
Mon. to Fri. 12 to 5, or by appointment.
1 block east of Larch, 1 block south of Shiawassee, in loft district just east of downtown.
Deco and modernism design.

12 Bob's Antiques
617 East Michigan
Lansing, MI
517 485-2177
Fri. & Sat. 10 to 4 by chance.
North side of street, just east of downtown.
Small shop.

13 Eberly's Emporium
3200 North East Street
Lansing , MI 48912
517 484-3355
By chance.
Northeast corner East Street & Community Street.

14 Classic Arms Company
1600 Lake Lansing Road
Lansing , MI 48912
517 484-6112
Mon. to Fri. 9 to 6, Sat. 9 to 5
One mile west of U.S. 127, south side of street.
Antique guns.

15 Pennyless in Paradise
1918 East Michigan
Lansing, MI 48912
517 485-8335
Tues. to Sat. 11 to 6, Mon. by appointment.
Southwest corner Michigan and Clemens Avenue.
Used furniture, some antiques.

16 Slightly Tarnished
2008 East Michigan
Lansing, MI 48912
517 485-3599
Mon. to Sat. 11 to 5:30
1/4 block west of Clemens Avenue, south side of street.
Used items, some antiques.

EAST LANSING

17 Prints Ancient & Modern
515 East Grand River Avenue
East Lansing, MI 48823
517 337-6366
Mon. to Wed. 10 to 6, Thurs. & Fri. 10 to 9, Sat. 10 to 5
Second floor.

18 Wooden Shoe Antique House
14944 Upton Road
East Lansing , MI 48823
517 641-6040
Mon. to Sat. 9 to 6; Sun. 1:30 to 5; or by appointment to 9
North of I-69; 1.5 miles north of Old M-78, west side of
Upton. Glass, China, primitives, old furniture.

OKEMOS

19 Sentimental Journey Antiques
1259 West Grand River
Okemos, MI 48864
517 349-1515
Mon. to Sat. 10 to 5:30, Thurs. to 8.
Upstairs in Wooden Skate Antiques.
Collective group of dealers; opened 1993.

20 Wooden Skate Antiques, Estate Jewelry & Gems
1259 W Grand River
Okemos , MI 48864
517 349-1515; FAX 517 349-8628
Mon. to Sat. 10 to 5:30, Thurs. to 8
Southwest corner Cornell Road & Grand River, 1.3 miles east of Meridian Mall, 6 miles west of Williamston.
Large facility; estate jewelry, Hummels, China, furnishings, etc.

21 Farm Village Antique Mall
3448 Hagadorn Road
Okemos , MI 48864
517 337-3266; 517 337-4988
Mon. to Sat. 11 to 6, Thurs. to 8; Sun 12 to 6
Southeast corner Hagadorn & Jolly Streets.
Very large multi-level facility, 35 dealers, 25,000 square feet.

22 Spud's Shop
3448 Hagadorn Road
Okemos, MI 48864
517 351-2140
Summer: Sat. & Sun. 1 to 5
Just outside Farm Village Antique Mall.

MASON

23 Mason Antiques Market
Mason Street
Mason , MI 48854
517 676-9753; 517 676-1270
Every day 10 to 6
Mason Antiques District

24 The Garment District
Mason Street
Mason , MI 48854
517 676-9753
7 Days 10 to 6
Mason Antiques District; upstairs from Mason Antique Market.
Vintage apparel.

25 The Carriage Shop
Mason Street
Mason , MI 48854
517 676-1530
Wed. to Sun. 10 to 6
Mason Antique District, in back of the Mason Antiques Market.
Toys, Dolls, Disney, Jewelry

26 Chapman's Old Mill Antiques Mall
207 Mason Street
Mason , MI 48854
517 676-1270
Every day 10 to 5
Mason Antique District

27 Front Porch Antiques
Mason Street
Mason , MI 48854
517 676-6388
Every day 10 to 6
Mason Antique District

28 The Loft Antiques Co-Op
Mason Street
Mason , MI 48854
517 676-0400
Wed. to Sun. 10 to 6
Mason Antique District, upstairs from The Front Porch.

29 Peddlers Row
Mason Street
Mason , MI 48854
No telephone.
Summer only: Every day 10 to 6
Mason Antique District
Outdoor sheds.

30 The Country House
Mason Street
Mason , MI 48854
517 676-1045
Wed. to Sun. 10 to 6
Mason Antique District

31 Rusty Nail Warehouse
Mason Street
Mason , MI 48854
No telephone.
Every day 10 to 6
Mason Antique District

32 Sally's Unique Jewelry & Antiques
(Formerly Lil & Sal's Antiques)
652 West Dexter Trail
Mason , MI 48854
517 676-1786
By chance.
2 1/2 miles southeast of Kipp Road, north side of road.
Barn in back of house.

LESLIE

33 Anns'tiques
4202 Meridian Road
Leslie , MI 49251
517 589-9225
March to Dec.: Wed., Fri. & Sat. 12 to 5
West side of road between Kinneville and Fitchburg Roads.
4 1/2 miles east of U.S. 127.

DANSVILLE

34 Red Barn Antiques & Collectibles
1131 Mason Street (M-36)
Dansville , MI 48819
517 623-6631
May 1 to Nov. 1: Fri. to Sun. 11 to 5
West edge of town, north side of street.

35 Right Up Town Resale Shop
1386 Mason Street
Dansville, MI 48819
517 623-6923
Mon. to Fri. 11 to 5
Downtown

STOCKBRIDGE

36 Tom Forshee Antiques
119 West Main Street
Stockbridge , MI 49285
517 851-8114
Fri. & Sat. 10 to 4; Sun. 12 to 4; or by appointment.
South side of street. Entrance from the rear parking lot enter from Wood Street southbound;at the red awning.
Oriental and English porcelains and American furniture.

37 White Oak Antiques
4665 East Cooper Road
Stockbridge , MI 49285
517 851-8151 Open by chance.
7 miles north of Stockbridge on M-52 (or 8 miles south of I-96), and one-half mile east of M-52.
Antiques and collectible junk.

WILLIAMSTON

38 Bittersweet Antiques
2200 Howell Road
Williamston, MI
517 655-1698 By chance or appointment.
South 6 miles on Williamston to T intersection with Howell Road; turn east; third house on south side of highway.
Country, quilts, depression glass, etc.

39 Gray Goose Antiques
150 South Putnam Street
Williamston , MI 48895
517 655-4043
Mon. to Sat. 10 to 5; Sun. by appointment.
Downtown, west side of street. 6 dealers; coop shop.

40 Lyon's Den Antiques
132 South Putnam Street
Williamston , MI 48895
517 655-2622
Wed. to Sat. 1 to 5, Sun. 12 to 5; Mon. & Tues. by chance
Downtown, west side of street, south of Grand River Ave.

41 Putnam Street Antiques
122 South Putnam Street, 2nd floor
Williamston , MI 48895
517 655-4521
Mon. to Sat 10:30 to 5; Sun. 12 to 4
Downtown, west side of street.
16 dealers.

42 Antique Shop
138 East Grand River Avenue
Williamston, MI 48895
517 655-6606
Wed. to Sun. 10 to 6
Downtown, south side of street.
6 dealers.

43 Happicats Antiques
133 East Grand River Avenue
Williamston , MI 48895
517 655-1251; 517 223-8039
Tues. to Sat. afternoons.
Downtown, north side of street.
Cat collectibles, vintage clothing, old books, and antiques.

44 Pieces of the Past
127 East Grand River
Williamston , MI 48895
517 655-3653
Tues. to Sun. 11 to 5
Downtown, north side of street.

45 Old Village Antiques
125 East Grand River Avenue
Williamston , MI 48895
517 655-4827
April thru Dec.: Tues. to Sat. 10 to 5, Sun. 12 to 5;
Jan. thru March: Fri. & Sat. 10 to 5, Sun. 12 to 5
Downtown, north side of street, east of light.
Wallace Nutting prints; Victorian furniture, art glass, etc.

46 Things Beer
100 East Grand River Avenue Downtown
Williamston, MI 48895
517 655-6701
Tues. to Fri. 12 to 7, Sat. 10 to 5; call Sun.
Beer brewing supplies & beer collectibles.

47 Corner Cottage
120 High Street
Williamston, MI 48895
517 655-3257
Wed. to Sat. 11 to 5; some Sundays.
Downtown, one block north of traffic light, just east of Putnam.
Refinished oak furniture, etc.

48 Legends Jewelry
104 West Grand River Avenue
Williamston, MI 48895
517 655-4221
Mon. to Sat. 10 to 5
Downtown
Estate jewelry.

49 Main Street Shoppe Antiques
108 West Grand River Avenue
Williamston, MI 48895
517 655-4005
Mon. to Sat. 10:30 to 5; Sun. 12 to 5
Downtown.
10 dealers.

50 Consignments of Williamston
115 West Grand River Avenue Downtown
Williamston, MI 48895
517 655-6064
Mon. to Sat. 10 to 6, Sun. 12 to 6
Antiques, collectibles, used things.

51 Old Plank Road Antiques
126 West Grand River Avenue
Williamston, MI 48895
517 655-4273
Summer: Tues. to Sat. 10 to 5 Winter: Tues. to Sat. 11 to 5
Downtown, north side of street.

52 The Vintage Years
540 West Grand River Avenue
Williamston, MI 48895
517 655-1340
Tues. to Sat. 10:30 to 5; Sun. by chance
Northeast corner Grand River Avenue & McCormick.
Books, dried flowers, antiques.

53 Poor Richard's Antiques
834 West Grand River Avenue
Williamston , MI 48895
517 655-2455
Wed. to Sat. 12 to 5
Northeast corner West Grand Avenue & Wint Street, eight blocks west of downtown. Costume jewelry, etc.

54 Grand River Merchants Antique Market
1039 West Grand River
Williamston , MI 48895
517 655-1350
Mon. to Sat. 10 to 5; Sun. 12 to 5:30
1 mile west of downtown stop light.
70 dealers, 15,000 square feet. Opened 1981.

WEBBERVILLE

55 Re-Use It Antiques, Consignments & Collectibles
120 West Grand River
Webberville, MI 48892
517 521-4390
Tues. to Sun. 10:30 to 5:30
Downtown, south side of street.

Note: Howell (Livingston County, east of Ingham County) has several antique shops and malls. They are listed in the *Complete Antique Shop Directory for Eastern Michigan*.

TIER 4: THE I-96 ROUTE

4.1 OTTAWA COUNTY

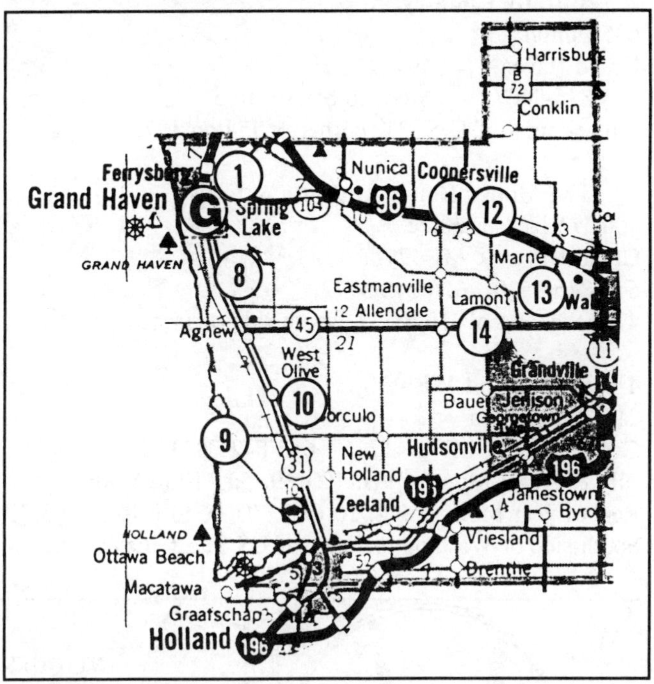

G: 2 to 7 - Grand Haven

Recommended Points of Interest:
* Tri-Cities Historical Museum, 1 N. Harbor, Grand Haven 616 842-0700

For Additional Information:
* Grand Haven-Spring Lake Visitors Bureau, 616 842-4499

SPRING LAKE

1 Spring Lake Antique Mall
801 W Savidge
Spring Lake , MI 49456
616 846-1774
Mon. to Sat. 10 to 6; Sun. 12 to 6
North side of road, just east of the Spring Lake bridge on M-104. 50 dealers. Glassware, furniture, collectibles.

GRAND HAVEN

2 Naturally Country
635 Fulton
Grand Haven, MI 49417
616 846-9467 Mon. to Sat. 10 to 5
1 block west of U.S. 31, corner of Fulton & 7th.

3 The Mouse House Antiques & Gifts
400 1/2 Jackson Street
Grand Haven , MI 49417
616 846-1530; 616 842-5772
4 blocks west off Hwy. 31, south side of Jackson.

4 Whims and Wishes
216 Washington
Grand Haven, MI 49417 616 842-9533
July & Aug.: Mon. to Fri. 10 to 9, Sat. 10 to 5:30;
Rest of year Mon. & Sat. 10 to 9; Tues. to Fri. 10 to 5:30
South side of Washington West of US 31. Gifts & antiques.

5 Raberne Cottage
Gallery Shops Complex, 107 Washington Street
Grand Haven, MI 49417
616 846-9260
Mon. to Sat. 10 to 5

6 Ad Lib
225 Franklin Street
Grand Haven, MI 49417
616 842-7300
Mon. to Sat. 10 to 5:30; Fri. to 9; + Sun. 12 to 5 summers
Downtown, Franklin is the 1st street s. of the main street.

7 Patricia's Glass and Antiques
100 S Beechtree St
Grand Haven , MI 49417
616 842-0781 Mon. to Sat. 10 to 5
Southeast corner Franklin & Beechtree.

8 West Michigan Antique Mall
13279 168th Street at U.S. 31 South
Grand Haven , MI 49417
616 842-0370
Mon. to Thurs. 10 to 5; Fri. & Sat. 10 to 7; Sun. 12 to 6
Entrance from 168th Avenue, just north of Ferris Street.
No entrance from U.S. 31. 12,000 square feet.

WEST OLIVE

9 Whispering Pines Antiques
6427 Butternut Drive
West Olive , MI 49460
616 399-6216
Thurs. 12 to 5; Fri. & Sat. 9 to 5
West 4 miles from U.S. 31 on Port Sheldon Street to
Butternut; shop is just to the north, west side of Butternut.

10 Lake Shore Antiques
10300 West Olive Road (U.S. 31)
West Olive , MI 49460
616 847-2429
Mon. to Sat. 10 to 6; Sun. 12 to 5
1.25 miles south of M-45, east side of highway. Not easily
visible to south-bound traffic due to trees in median.

COOPERSVILLE

11 Ye Olde Post Office
286 Ottawa Street
Coopersville , MI 49404
616 837-9475
Mon. to Fri. 10 to 5; Sat. 10 to 3; Nov. & Dec. Thur. to 8
East side of street between Main & Mechanic Streets, 1/2 block north of downtown light. Gifts, crafts, antiques.

12 Mostly Antiques
16694 48th Avenue
Coopersville , MI 49404
616 837-9695
Thurs., Fri. & Sat. 10 to 6; Sun. 12 to 5; or by chance.
East side of 48th Avenue, south of Cleveland.
Antiques, glassware, primitives, & collectibles.

LAMONT

13 Maple Valley Antiques
13575 42nd Avenue
Lamont (Marne) , MI 49430
616 677-3422
Mon. to Sat.: 10 to 6
Southwest corner Johnson & 42nd Avenue; north from the east edge of Lamont.
Country, primitives.

ALLENDALE

14 Ward's Antiques
5187 Lake Michigan Drive
Allendale , MI 49401
616-895-7015
Thur. to Sat. 10 to 5, or by appointment
North side of road, east of Allendale on M-45,just west of Grand Valley State University.
Advertising, Glassware, toys, jewelry.

4.1 Ottawa County - continued

15 Grand Valley Antique Mall
11233 68th Street
Allendale, MI 49401
616 892-6022
Mon. to Sat. 9 to 6, Sun. 12 to 5
Northwest corner 68th Street & M-45, in back of strip mall.
10,000 square feet; 45 dealers; opened 1993.

4.2 KENT COUNTY

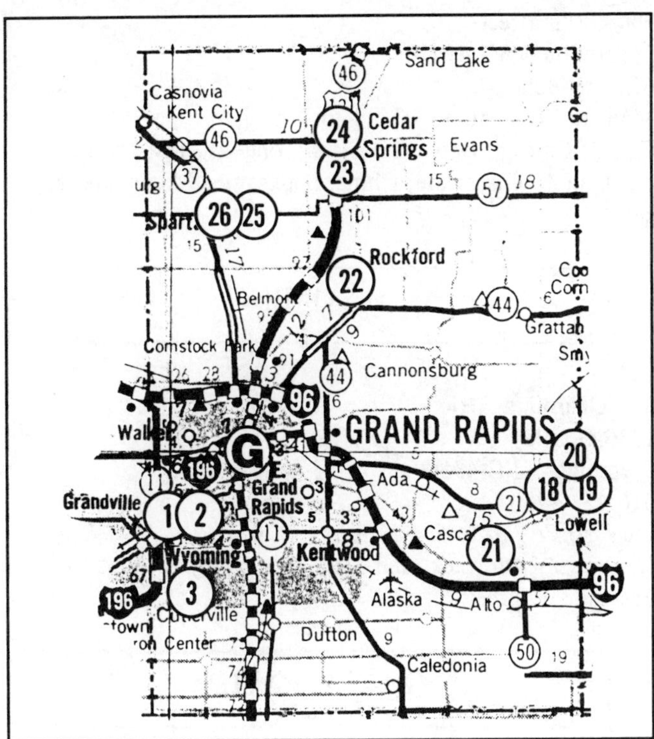

G: 4 to 17 - Grand Rapids, see Detail Map

Recommended Points of Interest:
* Heritage Hill Historic District, Grand Rapids
* Gerald Ford Museum, Grand Rapids, 616 456-2675
* Grand Rapids Public Museum, 616 456-3977
* 1895 Voight House, 115 College, 616 458-2422

For Additional Information:
* Kent County Visitors Bureau, 616 459-8287

GRANDVILLE

1 Memories - Antiques, Crafts, Collectables
2705 Sanford
Grandville, MI 49418
616 538-1010
Mon. to Sat. 10 to 6, Sun. 12 to 5
From I-96 exit at Grandville/Walker Exit, go east to Sanford Street, north on Sanford; mall is on the west side.

2 Yesterday's Treasures & Today's Joys
3948 30th Street
Grandville , MI 49418
616 249-8066
Mon. to Fri 11 to 5; Sat. 11 to 3
East of Chicago Drive & Wilson; one-way east-bound.
Small shop. Glassware; China; books; small knick knacks; etc.

WYOMING

3 Granny's Attic
1736 Godfrey SW
Wyoming , MI 49509
616 452-9250
Tues. to Fri. 10 to 6, Sat. 9 to 4;
Closed July 4th week, and Saturdays in July & Aug.
East side of street.

GRAND RAPIDS

4 Standale Country House Antiques and Reproductions
365 Cummings NW
Grand Rapids , MI 49504
616 453-7298
Mon. to Thur. 10 to 5:30; Fri. 10 to 8; Sat. 10 to 5:30
Near Brakes Plus, southwest corner of Cummings NW & Lake Michigan Dr.
Decorative accessories, reproductions, gifts, and some antiques.

4.2 Kent County - continued

GRAND RAPIDS DETAIL MAP

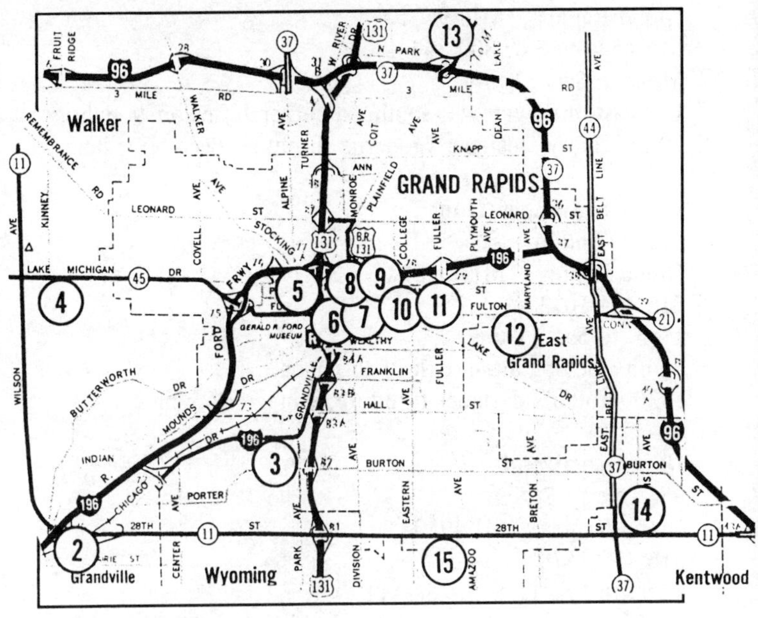

5 Antiques by the Bridge
445 Bridge N.W. (Michigan Street extended)
Grand Rapids , MI 49504
616 451-3430
Tue. to Sat. 10 to 5; Sun. 12 to 5
North side of street, just west of Broadway, west of river.
20 dealers, 9,000 square feet, 3 floors. One of the dealers, Mayfield Antiques, specializes in mission oak.

6 Perception
7 Ionia SW
Grand Rapids , MI 49503
616 451-2393
Mon. to Fri. 10 to 5:30; Sat. 10 to 2;
closed Sat. Memorial Day to Labor Day.
1 block south of Fulton, 2 blocks west of Division.
Art, some antiques.

7 Before & After Antiques
132 S. Division
Grand Rapids , MI 49503
616 458-4038 By appointment only.
Mid block between Oakes and Cherry, east side of street.
Mission oak, etc.

8 All Era
2 Jefferson SE.
Grand Rapids , MI 49501
616 454-9955 or 800 344-4868
Mon. to Sat. 12 to 6
Just east of downtown; southeast corner Jefferson & Fulton.
20th Century Designer Moderne furniture, decorative items.

9 A Scavenger Hunt
210 E. Fulton
Grand Rapids , MI 49503
616 454-1033
Mon. to Sat. 11 to 7
South side of Fulton, east of Jefferson.
1930's to 50's designer furniture; vintage clothing.

10 Heartwood
956 Cherry St SE
Grand Rapids , MI 49506
616 454-1478
Tues. to Fri. 11 to 5; Sat. 11 to 3
Southeast corner Cherry & Warren, just west of Diamond.
Mission; Art Deco; and other 20th Century decorative arts.

11 Nobody's Sweetheart Vintage
953 East Fulton
Grand Rapids , MI 49506
616 454-1673
Tues. to Sat. 12 to 6
North side of street, west of Diamond.
Antiques, collectibles, vintage clothing & costume jewelry.

12 Heirloom House Antiques
505 Lakeside Drive SE
East Grand Rapids , MI 49506
616 456-7094
Wed. to Sat. 11 to 4
3 miles east of downtown; NWC Creenwood & Lakeside.
Estate China, crystal, and art.

13 Apple Tree Antique Mall
3327 Plainfield NE
Grand Rapids , MI 49505
616 364-9730
Mon. 10 to 8; Tues. to Sat. 10 to 6; Closed Sundays.
In Apple Tree Mall, west side of Plainfield, near Wendy's.

14 Home Sweet Home Shop, Ltd.
3535 28th Street SE
Grand Rapids , MI 49512
616 949-7788
Mon. to Sat. 10 to 9
In Eastbrook Mall, at East Belt Line.
50% antiques, 50% new.

15 Plaza Antique Mall
1410 28th Street SE
Grand Rapids , MI 49506
616 243-2465
Mon. to Sat. 10 to 7; Sun. 1 to 5.
Southwest corner Kalamazoo Ave. & 28th Street.
68 dealers, 9,000 square feet.

16 Turn of the Century Antiques
(formerly Somewhere in Time Antiques)
7337 S. Division
Grand Rapids , MI 49508
616 455-2060
Mon. to Sat. 10 to 5
West side of street between 68th & 76th Streets.
Music boxes.

17 Koning's Wood Products
7226 S. Division
Grand Rapids , MI 49508
616 455-1780
Mon. to Fri. 9 to 5, Sat. 9 to 12
East side of the highway.

LOWELL

18 Flat River Antique Mall
212 W. Main St.
Lowell , MI 49331
616 897-5360
Sun. Mon. Tues. & Thurs. 10 to 6; Wed. & Fri. 10 to 8;
Sat. 9 to 6;
Downtown, south side of street.
Very large mall: 105 dealers, 35,000 square feet, 4 floors.

19 Cranberry Urn Antiques
208 E. Main
Lowell , MI 49331
616 897-9890; (616 897-9145 res.)
Tue. Wed. Fri. & Sat. 10 to 5
South side of street, east end of downtown; pull into the parking lot just east of the bridge.

20 Main Street Antique Mall
(Formerly the site of Aunt Annabell Bean Antiques)
221 W. Main Street
Lowell , MI 49331
616 897-5521
Downtown, north side of street.
Wed. to Fri. 11 to 6; Sat. & Sun. 11 to 5
10 dealers, 3,600 square feet.

21 Unique Shop
11231 Grand River Dr SE
Lowell , MI 49331
616 897-7085
Daily 11 to 5; Closed Thurs. & Sun.
From west end of downtown cross the Grand River on Alden Nash Road, take an immediate right down Grand River Drive; shop is blue house with white roof two miles down on right side.
Crafts, country items, & general line.

ROCKFORD

22 Salli & Friends Antique Mall
124 N Main St
Rockford , MI 49341
616 866-3301
Tues. to Sat. 11 to 5; Sun 12 to 5
Downtown, east side of street.
15 dealers, 2,000 square feet.

CEDAR SPRINGS

23 Red Flannel Antique Co.
128 North Main Street
Cedar Springs , MI 49319
616 696-9599
Daily 11 to 5, Fri. till 7; closed Monday
Downtown on Old Route 46, east side of street.

24 Cedar Springs Antiques
288 North Main Street
Cedar Springs , MI 49319
616 696-0756
Mon. to Sat. 9 to 5
East side of Main (Old M-46) one-half block north of Pine Street.

SPARTA

25 Rogue River Antiques
476 East Division
Sparta, MI 49345
616 887-2525
Mon., Tues., Thurs. & Fri. 10 to 5, Sat. 10 to 3,
Sun. 1 to 4
3 blocks east of downtown, south side of street.

26 Apple Town Antiques Mall
112 East Division
Sparta, MI 49345
616 887-5173
Tues. to Thurs. 11 to 5, Fri. & Sat. 11 to 8, Sun. 1 to 5
Downtown, southwest corner main intersection.

4.3 IONIA COUNTY

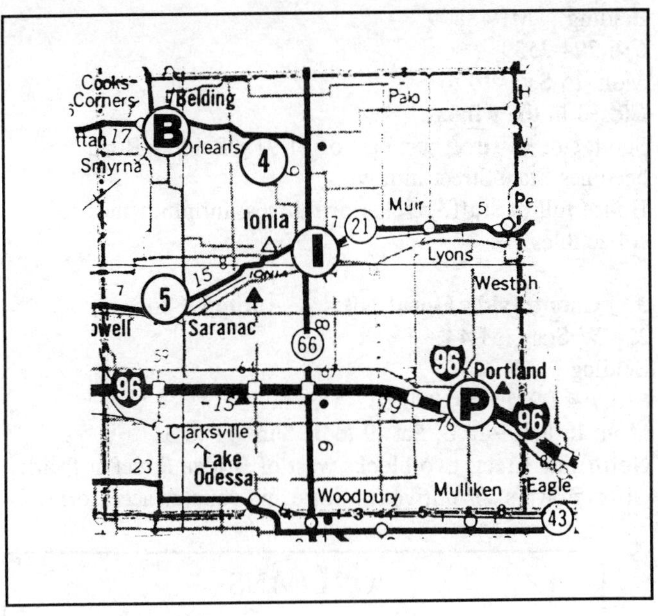

B: 1 to 3 - Belding
I: 6 to 9 - Ionia
P: 12 to 15 - Portland

For Additional Information:
* Ionia Chamber of Commerce, 616 527-2560

BELDING

1 Mari-Mar Sales
1439 W State (M-44)
Belding , MI 48809
616 794-2423
Mon. to Wed. and Fri. & Sat. 10 to 5
Red barn set back from road; south side of M-44 between Bridge St. & M-91
Furniture; glassware; dolls; jewelry and collectibles.

2 P.S. Antiques & Collectibles
9173 W Belding Road (M-44)
Belding , MI 48809
616 794-2559
Mon. to Sat. 10 to 5;
Closed in the winter.
South side of street just east of M-91. Belding Road becomes State Street in town.
House full of stuff: clocks; primitives; furniture and collectibles.

3 Countryside Floral Gifts & Antique Shop
224 W State (M-44)
Belding , MI 48809
616 794-0921 or 1-800 842-3137
Mon. to Fri. 9 to 6; Sat. 9 to 4; Sun. 11 to 3
North side street, two blocks west of Bridge Street at Pearl.
Gifts, flowers, primitive furniture and country accessories.

ORLEANS

4 Village Antique Shop
Next to Post Office
Orleans, MI 48865
Tues. to Sat.
3 miles west of M-66, 1/2 mile south of M-44.

SARANAC

5 Saranac Antique Exchange
28 Vosper
Saranac , MI 48881
616 642-6291
Open 7 Days: Mon. thru Sat. 10 to 6; Sun. 1:30 to 5:30.
2 blocks east of downtown at 28 Vosper Street in a vintage school building.

IONIA

6 Ionia Antique Mall
415 West Main
Ionia , MI 48846
616 527-6720
Mon. to Sat.: 10 to 5, Fri. to 9, Sun. 12 to 5
Downtown, south side of the street 1/2 block from M-66.

7 Lehman's Antiques & Collectibles
401 West Main Street
Ionia , MI 48846
616 527-2844
Mon. Tues. Wed. Fri. & Sat. 10 to 5; Thurs. & Sun. 12 to 5
Downtown, at the corner of Main & Steele Streets.

8 Fire Barn Antiques
219 West Washington Street
Ionia, MI 48446
616 527-2240
Mon., Tues., Thurs., & Sat. 10 to 5; Wed. 4 to 7; Fri. 10 to 7; Sun. 12 to 5
South side of street, next to Post Office, 1 block off Main.

9 Checkerboard Antiques
524 West Lincoln
Ionia, MI 48846
616 527-1785
Open every day 10 to 6
North of Downtown, north side of street.

10 Grand River Country Mall
7050 South State
Ionia , MI 48846
616 527-8880
Every Day 10 to 5, Fri. to 9
M-66 1/4 mile north of I-96 Exit 67, west side of highway.

PORTLAND

11 McMillen & Wife Antiques
9073 South State Road
Portland , MI 48875
616 374-8088
Wed. to Sun. 10 to 5
M-66 & Goodemonte Road, 1 1/4 mile south of I-96 Exit 67, west of Portland, south of Ionia.

12 Lost in Time Antiques & Collectibles
131 Kent Street
Portland, MI 48875
517 647-9961
Every Day 12 to 5
Downtown, across from Amy's Restaurant.

13 Robinson's Antiques
170 Kent Street
Portland , MI 48875
517 647-6155
Usually: Mon. to Fri. 9 to 5; Sun. 11 to 4
Downtown
Antique furniture hardware, house hardware, etc.

14 Portland Flea Market
143 Kent Street
Portland , MI 48875
517 647-4484
Sat. 9 to 6, Sun. 9 to 5
Downtown
Antiques, old stuff & reproductions.

15 Oaks
344 Lincoln Street
Portland , MI 48875
517 647-4604
Open by chance.
Go south from downtown on Kent 2 blocks to Brush, east on Brush 5 blocks to Lincoln.

16 Farmers Barn
9479 Okemos Road
Portland , MI 48875
517 647-7684
Sat. & Sun. 12 to 6; Weekdays by chance or appointment.
South from Portland on Charlotte 1 mile to Peake, west on Peake 1/4 mile to end of road, north on dead end dirt road 1/2 mile.
Large shed with lots of furniture in-the-rough & miscellaneous.

17 McMillen & Husband
11464 McCrumb Road
Portland , MI 48875
517 627-2794
Sat. & Sun. 10 to 5, weekdays by chance.
Southeast from Portland 1 mile to Frost, south on Frost 1 1/2 miles to McCrumb, east on McCrumb 1/4 mile.
Teddy bears, dolls, pottery, art glass, etc.

4.4 CLINTON COUNTY

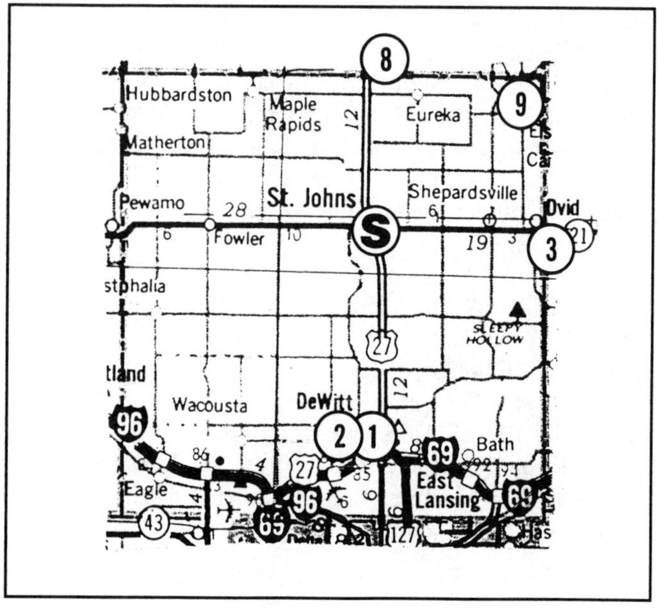

S: 4 to 7 - St. Johns

Recommended Points of Interest:
* Clinton Co. Historical Society, St. Johns, 517 224-2894

For Additional Information:
* St. Johns Chamber of Commerce, 517 224-7248

DeWITT

1 Ely's Collectibles
126 North Bridge
DeWitt , MI 48820
517 669-9048 Open by appointment.
Downtown, southeast corner Bridge & Jefferson Streets.
Primitives, books.

2 Grumpy Bear Antiques
113 West Main Street
DeWitt, MI 48820
517 669-2327
Thurs. to Sun. 11 to 6

OVID

3 My Little Shop
9950 East M-21
Ovid, MI 48866
517 834-2520
Tues. to Sat. 11 to 5, Sun. 12 to 4:30
South side of highway, 1/2 mile east of Ovid.
Primitives, flea market items, etc.

ST. JOHNS

4 Wildflower Antiques
800 East State Street
St. Johns, MI 48879
517 224-6505
Mon. to Fri. 1 to 6
State is the street on the south side of the Court House; 2 blocks east of Business U.S. 27.

5 Irrer Antiques
201 West McConnell
St. Johns, MI 48879
517 224-4085
Every Day 11 to 6, or by appointment.
White house, southwest corner Church & McConnell Streets; 7 blocks west of 27 or 2 blocks south of 21.

6 Antiques & Collectibles
601 West Cass Street
St. Johns, MI 48879
517 224-3864
Mon. to Sat. 11 to 6, or by appointment.
Cass is the street north of the Court House.
Small shop in garage attached to house.

7 Jerry Nickel Antiques
1300 N. Lansing Street
St. Johns , MI 48879
517 224-6248
By appointment.
3 blocks west of Clinton, north of town.

8 County Line Antiques
2021 S County Line Rd
St. Johns , MI 48879
517 224-6285, res: 517 838-2526
Thurs. to Mon. 10 to 5:30
Northeast corner U.S. 27 & County Line Road, 8 miles north of St. Johns.
Nice general line of antiques.

ELSIE

9 Melvin's Antiques & Clock Shop
8401 Island Road
Elsie, MI 48831
517 862-4322
Daily 10 to 8 by chance or appointment.
3/4 mile west of stoplight on West Main Street.

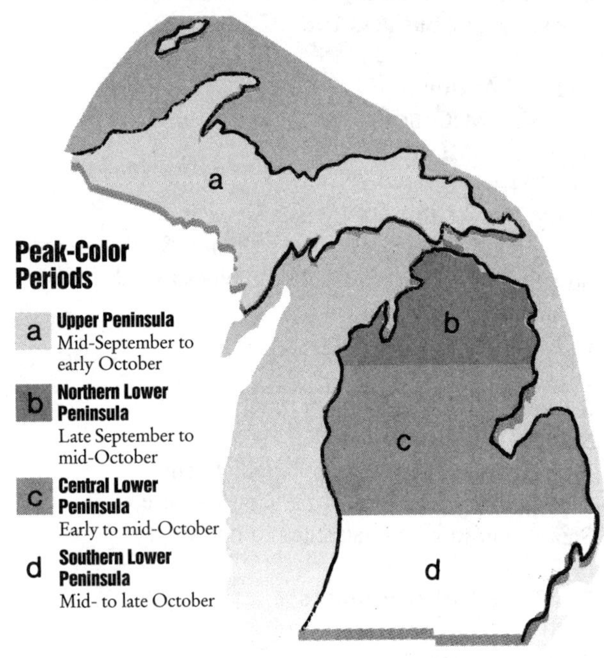

TIER 5
THE M-46 ROUTE

5.1 MUSKEGON

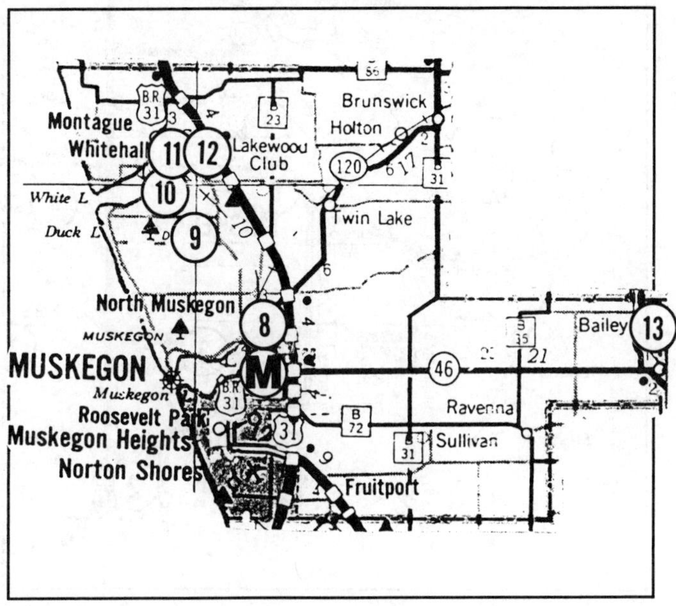

M: 1 to 7 - Muskegon, see Detail Map

Recommended Points of Interest:
* Hackley & Hume Houses, 484 W. Webster, 616 722-7578
* Muskegon Museum of Art, 616 722-7578

For Additional Information:
* Muskegon Visitors Bureau, 616 722-3751

MUSKEGON

1. Cloverville Mall
3169 Heights Ravenia Road
Muskegon , MI 49442
616 773-5703
Mon. to Sat. 10:30 to 6, Sun. 12 to 5
From I-96 go north on U.S. 31 2 miles to Sherman (County B72); go east two miles; mall is at SEC Dangel Road. Antiques, collectibles, crafts.

5.1 Muskegon County - continued

MUSKEGON DETAIL MAP

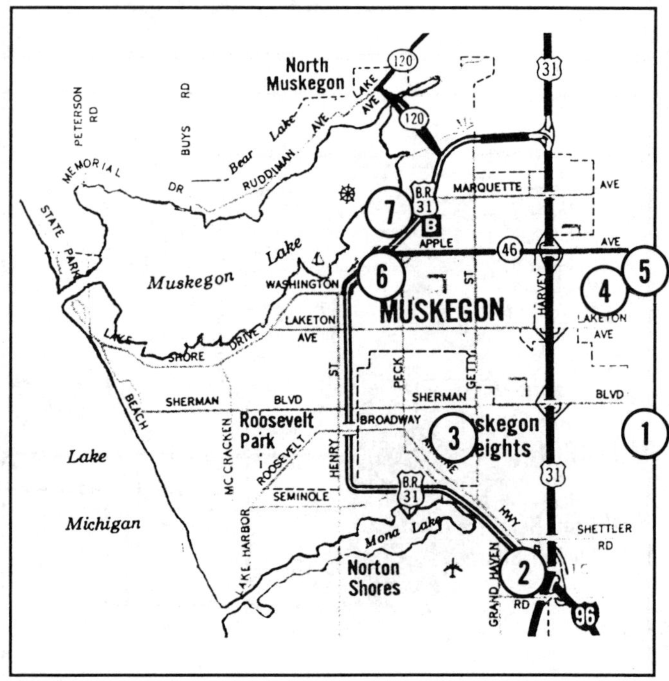

2 Airport Antique Mall
4206 Grand Haven Road
Muskegon (Norton Shores), MI 49441
616 798-3318
Mon. to Sat. 11 to 6; Sun. 12 to 6
South from Muskegon on Business U.S. 31, exit on Grand Haven Road; the mall is several blocks south at the southeast corner of Airport Road.
Mostly glassware & smalls. 25 dealers, 5,000 square feet.

3 Strippers of Muskegon
3535 Getty
Muskegon , MI 49441
616 733-2201 Open by chance.
South of Sherman Street, west side of street.

4 Mandy's Antiques
1950 E Laketon Ave
Muskegon , MI 49441
616 777-1428
Mon. to Fri. 1 to 4; Sat. 10:30 to 3
2 blocks east of US 31, north side of street at Port City Rd.

5 Old Grange Mall
2783 Apple Avenue
Muskegon, MI 49442
616 773-5683
Tues. to Sat. 10 to 5
1.5 miles east of U.S. 31, southwest corner Walker Road.
Set up like an old country store.

6 Belasco's Antiques
1391 Peck St
Muskegon , MI 49441
616 726-3689
Tues. to Fri. 12 to 5; Sat. 9 to 1
West side of Peck Street at Irwin Street.

7 Downtown Muskegon Antique Mall
East Clay & Cedar, U.S. Business 31
Muskegon , MI 49442
616 728-0305
Mon. to Thurs. 10 to 5; Fri. & Sat. 10 to 7; Sunday 1 to 5
Just west of Business U.S. 31, north end of downtown, at East Clay & Cedar Streets.
60 dealers, 6,000 square feet.

NORTH MUSKEGON

8 Memory Lane Antique Mall
2073 Holton Road
North Muskegon , MI 49445
616 744-8510
Every Day 10 to 6
Northwest corner M-120 & U.S. 31 Expressway.
37 dealers, 6,000 square feet.
Opened in 1992.

9 Country Peddler Antiques
2542 West Bard Road
North Muskegon, MI 49445
616 766-2147
Wed., Fri. & Sat. 11 to 5, Thurs. 3 to 8
North on Whitehall Road 4 miles from North Muskegon, west on Bard 2 miles; north side of the street.
Crafts & antiques.

WHITEHALL

10 Martha's Vineyard Antiques
4075 Lakewood Road
Whitehall , MI 49461
616 894-6602
May 1 through October: 12 to 5 daily
Southeast corner Zeller Street & Lakewood Road.
Barn in the back yard.

11 Slocum Street Antiques
116 W. Slocum
Whitehall , MI 49461
616 893-0798
By chance.
2 blocks south of Colby (the main street), between Mears & Lake Michigan.
Toys etc.

12 White Lake Antique Mall
103 East Colby Street
Whitehall , MI 49461
616 893-1244
Mon. to Sat. 10 to 6; Sun. 12 to 5
Downtown. Large paved parking lot in back, with rear entrance to mall.
30 dealers, 6,000 square feet, 2 floors.

BAILEY

13 The Tin Man
1414 Newaygo Road
Bailey , MI 49303
616 834-7141
Thurs. 9 to 4; Fri. to Sun. 9 to 5
Northeast corner M-37 & Bailey Road, 3 miles south of Grant.
Small shop with new & used items, lawn ornaments, & antiques.

5.2 MONTCALM COUNTY

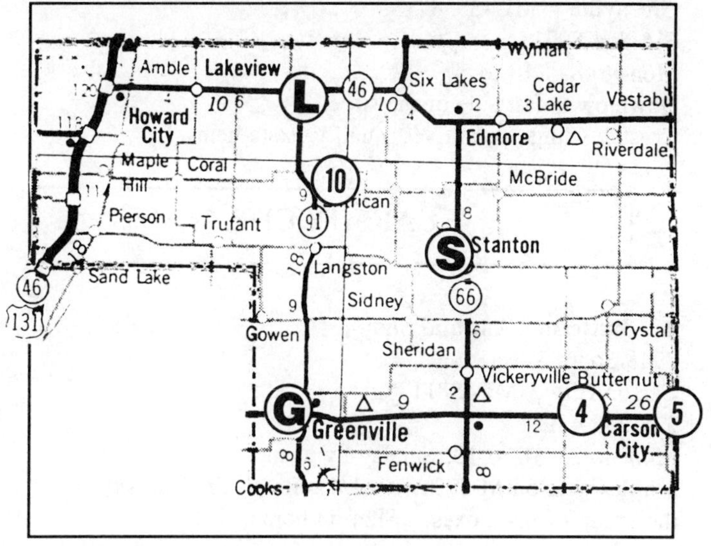

G: Greenville - 1 to 3
S: Stanton - 6 to 9
L: Lakeview - 12 to 14

For Additional Information:
* Greenville Chamber of Commerce, 616 754-5697

GREENVILLE

1 Greenville Antique Center
404 South LaFayette Street
Greenville , MI 48838
616 754-5540
Sun. to Wed. 11 to 6, Thurs. & Fri. 11 to 8, Sat. 10 to 8
Just south of downtown; loft building on east side of street.
Parking just south of the building. 5 floors, 15,000 sq. ft.

2 T & L Antiques Mall
123 S Lafayette St
Greenville , MI 48838
616 754-5960 or 616 794-2273 for appointments
Mon. Tues. Thurs. Fri. 10:30 to 5; Sat. 10 to 5
Downtown, west side of the street.
50 % antiques and 50 % new oak reproductions.

3 Red Pump Antiques
110 S Lafayette
Greenville , MI 48838
616 754-8991
Mon. to Sat. 10 to 5
Downtown, east side of the street.
Crystal, China, primitives, quality estate items.

CARSON CITY

4 Butternut Antique Shop
7948 South Street
Carson City , MI 48811
517 235-4398
Mon. to Sat 10 to 10; Sunday by chance
3 miles west on M-57, north 1/4 mile on Crystal, west at the group of mailboxes. Shop in home.

5 Cook's Crossing Antiques
105 W Main St
Carson City , MI 48811
517 584-6105; 517 235-4673
Tues. to Sat. 10 to 4; to 6 on Wed.
Downtown, west of Division & M-57, next to S&N Pizza.

STANTON

6 Antique Stuff
2990 1/2 Sheridan Road
Stanton , MI 48888
517 831-8063; 800 572-6703
Mon. to Sat. 10 to 5; Sun. by chance; Fri. & Sat. by chance April to Oct.
3 miles south of Stanton or NWC M-66 and Sidney Road.

7 Grapevine Treasures
105 Main Street
Stanton , MI 48888
517 831-8115, or 517 235-4220
Mon. Thurs. & Fri. 12 to 6; Sat. 10 to 3, or by aptmt.
Downtown, north side of street.
8 dealers. Antiques & household items.

8 Hotel Montcalm
106 Camburn
Stanton, MI 48888
517 831-5055
Every Day 12 to 6
Downtown, Main Street (M-66) & Camburn Street.

9 West Shore Antiques
1081 W Clifford Lake Dr
Stanton , MI 48888
517 831-4457
May to Sept.: Daily 10 to 6, or by appointment.
1/4 miles north of the Clifford Lake Hotel on Clifford Lake.
General line, plus depression glass.

VESTABERG

10 Ora Deila Antiques
9881 Cannonsville
Vestaburg , MI 48891
517 268-5143
By chance or appointment.
South on Crystal 5 miles from M-46; east .8 mile, south side of road.

SIX LAKES

11 The Potato Been
3572 W Fleck Rd
Six Lakes , MI 48886
517 365-3477
Summer: Tues. through Sun. 1 to 5; closed Dec. 24 to Feb.; Winter: Limited hours, Call first.
One block west of downtown, north side of street. Fleck Road between M-66 and M-46 is unpaved.
Large place filled with lots of stuff.

LAKEVIEW

12 Antiques - Dolls
7177 M-46
Lakeview , MI 48850
517 352-6393 Open by chance or appointment.
Southeast corner M-46 & Fitzner Street.

13 Granny's Antiques
9535 Fitzner Rd
Lakeview , MI 48850
517 352-6030
By chance or appointment.
NWC M-46 & Fitzner, 1.5 miles east of Lakeview.
Glassware, China, pottery and jewelry.

14 Tara II Antiques and Stuff
531 Lincoln
Lakeview , MI 48850
616 937-5148 Res.
Fri. 11 to 4; Sat. 11 to 3; Mon. Tues. & Thurs. by chancc.
Northeast corner Fifth & Lincoln, large blue house.

AMBLE

15 Amble Antiques and Collectibles
14766 M-46
Amble , MI 49322
616 762-4548
Mon. to Fri. 12 to 6, Sat. by chance.
North side of highway just east of Amble Road.

HOWARD CITY

16 Haack's Antiques
413 Muenscher
Howard City , MI 49329 616 937-4494
Always open. Knock on house door if shop is closed.
Old US 31 south from downtown two blocks to Chestnut,
west over the tracks on Chestnut to Muenscher, then south.

5.3 GRATIOT COUNTY

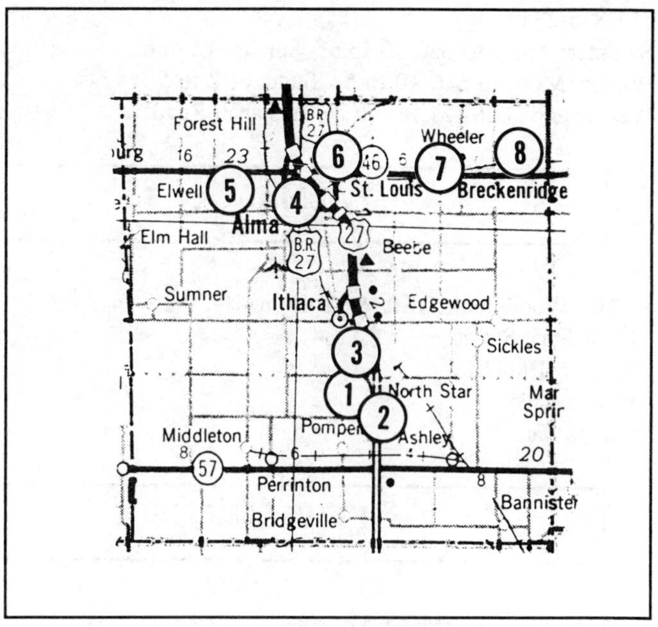

ITHACA

1 My Sister's Closet
1355 E. Grant Road
Ithaca , MI 48847
517 838-4096
Summer: Every day 10 to 6;
Winter: Every day 10 to 5
West side of U.S. 27, 5 miles south of Buchanan Road, 2 miles north of M-57.
Gifts, glassware, pottery

2 North Star Trader
3036 South Bagley Road, U.S. 27
Ithaca , MI 48847
517 875-4341 or 517 838-4409
Daily 11 to 5; closed Wed.
West side of highway, 3 miles south of Ithaca.
Used furniture, oak reproductions, & antiques; 25 % of the items are antiques.

3 Countryside Antiques
2024 South Bagley, U.S. 27
Ithaca , MI 48847
517 875-2349
Summer: Mon. to Sat. 10 to 6, Sunday 12 to 6;
Winter: Mon. to Sat. 10 to 5, Sunday 12 to 5
West side of U.S. 27, north of Buchanan Road.

ALMA

4 The Woodstock Gifts & Antiques
317 S. State Street
Alma, MI 48801
517 463-6425
Mon. to Sat.

ELWELL

5 Mac Lachlan House Antiques
6482 N Pingree Rd
Elwell , MI 48832
517 463-1512
May to December: Sat. & Sun. 12 to 5; or by appointment.
Downtown, southeast corner Kates Drive & Pingree Road.
Vintage radio and phonograph items, etc.

ST. LOUIS

6 Mary's Memories
603 East Washington
St. Louis , MI 48880
517 681-2286
Wed. to Fri. 10 to 5; Sat. 10 to 2
North side of street between Euclid and Hubbard, east side of St. Louis. There is a turn-around in front of the shop.

BRECKENRIDGE

7 BJ's Antiques & Coins
222 Saginaw
Breckenridge , MI 48615
517 842-5572
Mon. to Fri. 9 to 5; Sat. 9 to 3
Downtown, next to Village Pro Hardware, south side of street.

WHEELER

8 Auntie Q's
8150 N. Mason
Wheeler, MI 48662
517 842-5862
Summer: Mon. to Sat. 10 until dark, Sun. 11 until dark;
Winter: Tues. to Sat. 10 to 5, Sun. 11 to 5.
Northeast corner Mason Road & M-46 between Merrill and Breckenridge.

TIER 6
THE M-20 ROUTE

6.1 OCEANA COUNTY

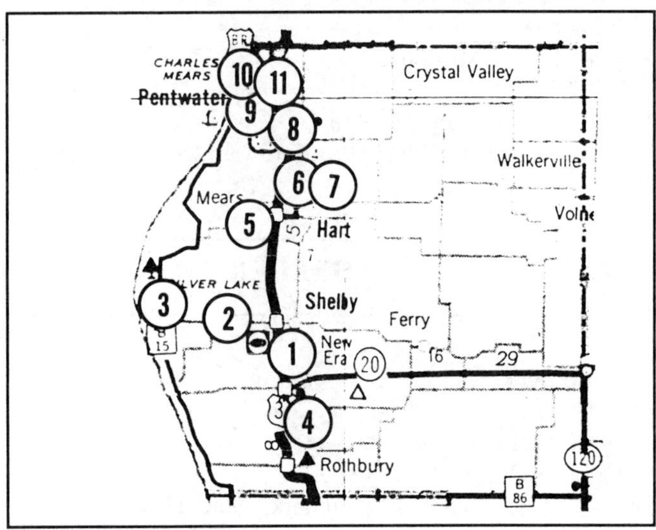

Recommended Points of Interest:
* Oceana County Historical Museum, Shelby, 616 861-2965

For Additional Information:
* Pentwater Chamber of Commerce, 616 869-4150

SHELBY

1 Nielsen's Nest
1021 S. Oceana Dr. (Old U.S. 31)
Shelby , MI 49455
616 861-4920
10 to 5 Daily; Closed Sunday; Thurs. by chance.
1/2 mile north of Shelby, west side of the highway.

2 Ruby's Antiques
6410 West Shelby Road
Shelby , MI 49455
616 861-4409
Fri. to Sun. 12 to 5; other times by chance.
4.5 miles west of Shelby, NWC 48th Avenue & Shelby Rd.

3 The Barn Antiques
15 S. 24th Avenue
Shelby , MI 49455
616 861-5038
Spring to Fall: Weekends & holidays 10 to 5;
Off-season & weekdays by chance.
7 miles west of U.S. 31to 24th Avenue, north 2.5 miles.
Large barn with antiques & home decor items.

ROTHBURY

4 Oceana Antique Mall
Old 31 & Cleveland
Rothbury , MI 49452
616 861-4993
Thurs. to Sun. 10:30 to 6
1.5 miles north of Rothbury, SEC Cleveland & Old U.S. 31
12 dealers.

MEARS

5 Remains to be Seen
56th & Taylor
Mears , MI 49436
616 873-3052
Open by chance.
Northeast corner Taylor & 56th Avenue, just south of Mears. Exit U.S. 31 at Polk Road, west 1 mile, south 1.5 miles through Mears. Shed attached to house.

HART

6 Courtland House
16 Courtland Street
Hart , MI 49420
616 873-4746
Summer: Mon. to Fri. 10 to 5; Sat. 10 to 4; Winter: Sat. 10 to 4
1 block west of Washington & Main intersection.
Antiques, crafts, vintage clothing.

7 The Flower Bin
27 South State Street
Hart, MI 49420
616 873-0222
Mon. to Sat. 10 to 6;
Memorial Day to Labor Day also open Sun. 10 to 5
Downtown
Flowers and antiques.

8 Four Generations
R-2 Monroe Road
Hart , MI 49420
616 873-2747
April & May & Sept. & Oct.: Sat. & Sun. 12 to 5;
June to Aug.: Fri. to Sun. 12 to 5
South side of road between U.S. 31 and Old 31, midway between Hart and Pentwater.

PENTWATER

9 The Berry Patch
210 South Hancock
Pentwater, MI 49449
616 869-5152
June & Sept.: Mon. to Sat. 10 to 5, Sun. 12 to 5;
July & Aug.: Mon. to Sat. 10 to 9, Sun. 12 to 5
Downtown
Gifts & antiques.

10 Oldewick Post
134 South Hancock
Pentwater , MI 49449
616 869-4322
Mon. to Sat. 10 to 5, Sun. 12 to 5
Downtown
Gifts, fudge, expresso, and antiques.

11 First Street Antiques
First Street & Hancock Street
Pentwater, MI 49449
616 869-5745
Most days 10 to 5:30.
Downtown, 1/4 block east of Hancock Street.

6.2 NEWAYGO COUNTY

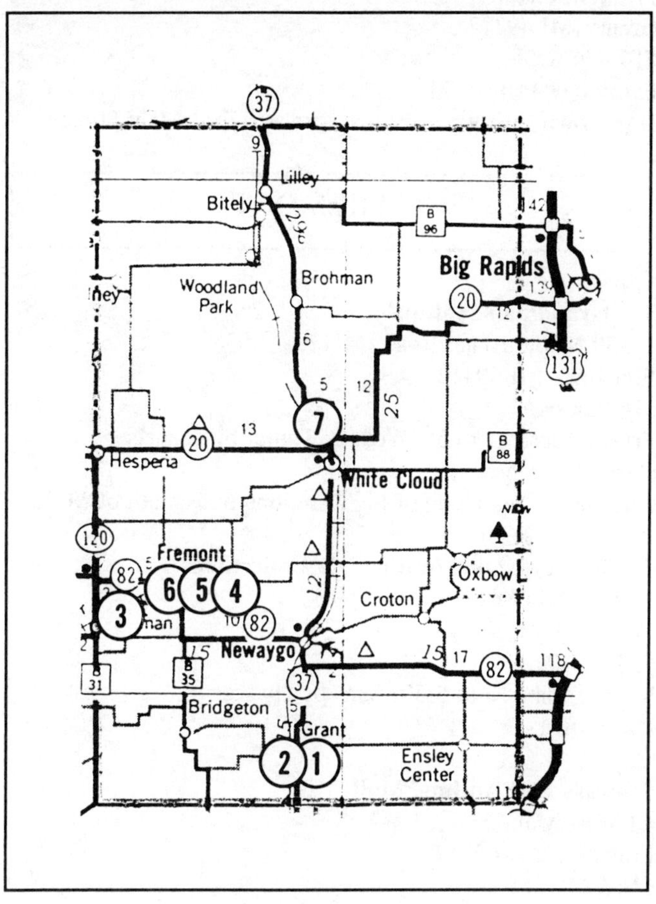

For Additional Information:
* White Cloud Chamber of Commerce, 616 689-6607

GRANT

1 Main Street Antique Mall
21 West Main Street
Grant, MI 49327
616 834-9846
Summer: Mon. to Sat. 10 to 6; Winter to 5:30
Downtown, north side of street.
Opened 1994

2 Grant Antique Mall
77 Front Street
Grant, MI 49227
616 834-6255
Every day 11 to 5:30
Downtown, just west of the tracks at end of Main Street.

FREMONT

3 Grandma's Antiques
10330 Maple Island Road (M-120)
Fremont, MI 49412
616 924-6467
Fri. to Tues. 11 to 5; Wed. & Thurs. by chance;
closed Sun. in winter.
Farm house, east side of highway, one mile south of M-82.

4 The Newsstand Antiques & Collectibles
14 W. Main Street
Fremont, MI 49412
616 924-0420
Mon. to Sat. 10 to 5:30. Sun. by chance.
Downtown

5 Brass Bell Antique Mall
48 West Main
Fremont, MI 49412
616 924-1255
Mon. to Sat. 10 to 5:30, Sun. 12 to 5; closed Sun. Jan. to March
Downtown, south side of street.

6 Linger Longer Antique Mall
1003 West Main Street (M-82)
Fremont, MI 49412
616 924-3318
Mon. to Thurs. 9 to 5:30, Fri. 9 to 7, Sat. 9 to 5, Sun. 12 to 5
5 miles east of M-120, near Lee's Chicken & Amoco.

WHITE CLOUD

7 R & E Variety
(aka Rosy Green's Antiques)
901 North Evergreen (M-37)
White Cloud , MI 49349
616 689-5849 or 689-6121
Summer: Daily 9 to 5, closed Tues. & Wed.;
Winter: Thurs. to Mon. 10 to 5
One mile north of White Cloud, west side of highway.

(616) 689-6121
(616) 689-5849

R & E Variety

DEPRESSION GLASS • FURNITURE
ANTIQUES • COLLECTIBLES • MISCELLANEOUS ITEMS
WE BUY ESTATES
OPEN THURSDAY THROUGH MONDAY 10 AM TO 5 PM

ROSETTA GREEN
WHITE CLOUD, MI 49349

ON M-37
ONE MILE NORTH OF TOWN

MAP OF MECOSTA COUNTY:

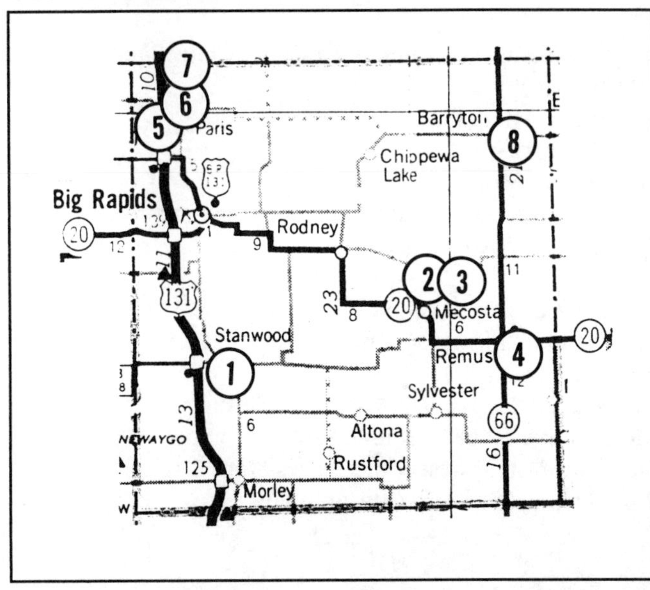

6.3 MECOSTA COUNTY

Map on Preceding Page

For Additional Information:
* Mecosta Visitors Bureau, 616 796-7640

STANWOOD

1 Treasures Unlimited
24 South Front Street
Stanwood , MI 49346
616 823-2495
Wed. to Sat. 10 to 5; Tues. & Sun. by chance.
East side of street, one block east of Old 131.
Resale shop with some glassware and pictures.

MECOSTA

2 The Tamarack Shoppe Crafts & Collectiques
699 W. Main
Mecosta , MI 49332
616 972-4222
Fri., Sat. & Mon 10 to 5; Sun. 12 to 5
West of downtown, southeast corner Franklin Street.
Quilts, glassware, crafts etc.

\3 The Browse Around
301 W. Main Street (M-20)
Mecosta , MI 49332
616 972-2990; 616 972-8103
Mon. to Sat. 10 to 5, Sun. 12 to 5
Downtown, southwest corner James Street
7 dealers; antiques and used furniture.

REMUS

4 Hilltop Heirlooms (The Barn)
231 E Wheatland
Remus , MI 49340
517 967-3402
May 1 to Nov. 1: Daily 8 to 5;
East on M-20, big barn on north side of the road.

PARIS

5 Todd's Antiques
23419 22 Mile Road
Paris , MI 49338
616 832-5026
Mon. to Fri. 12 to 5; Weekends by chance.
North on Northland Drive (Old 131) from Big Rapids to Paris; west on 22 Mile Road 2.5 miles, south side of road.

6 R. & M. Log Cabin
22920 Northland Drive (Old 131)
Paris, MI 49338
616 832-2941
Tues. to Sun. 10 to 6, Sun. 10 to 6
Half mile north of Paris, east side of highway.

7 Paris Country Shop
22203 Northland Drive (Old U.S. 131)
Paris , MI 49338
616 832-4533
Tues. to Sun. 12 to 5 West side of highway.

BARRYTON

8 The Hodgepodge
19120 30th Avenue (M-66)
Barryton, MI 49305
517 382-5526
Mon. to Sat. 8 to 6, Sun. 10 to 5
Antiques, collectibles, Coca Cola collectibles.

6.4 ISABELLA COUNTY

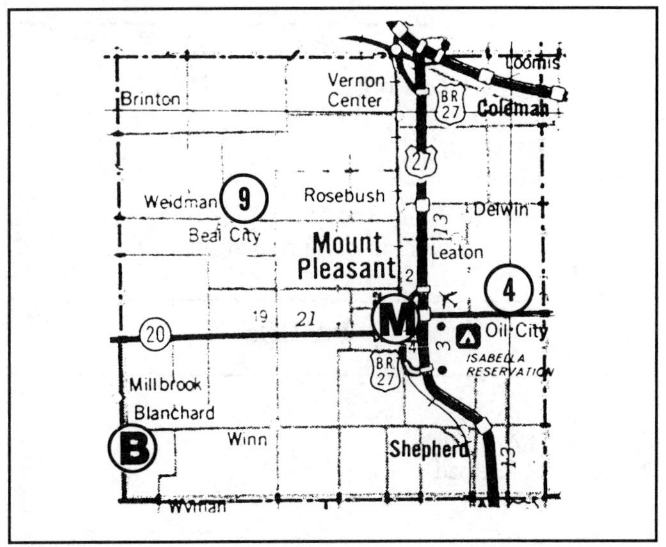

B: 1 to 3 - Blanchard
M: 5 to 8 - Mount Pleasant, see Detail Map

Recommended Points of Interest:
* Center for Cultural & Natural History, 517 774-3829

For Additional Information:
* Isabella County Visitors Bureau, 517 772-4433

BLANCHARD

1 The Wooden Sleigh
333 W Main
Blanchard, MI 49310
517 268-5045 or 517 561-5115
Mon. thru Sat. 10 to 5.
Located in Calico Corners, Downtown Blanchard.

2 Johnson's Junque
424 Main Street
Blanchard , MI 49310
517 561-2075
April to Dec.: Thurs. to Sat 10 to 5
South side of street, east end of downtown.

3 Loafer's Glory
431 Main Street
Blanchard , MI 49310
517 561-2020; (517 831-4264 res.)
April to Dec.: Tues. to Sat. 10 to 5;
Feb. & Mar.: Thurs. to Sat. 10 to 4; Closed Jan.
Downtown, north side of street.
Most antiques are on the second floor.

MOUNT PLEASANT

4 Schoolhouse Antiques
8995 East Pickard (M-20)
Mt. Pleasant , MI 48858
517 772-4660
May to Dec.: Fri. to Mon. 12 to 5;
Jan. to April: Fri. to Sun. 12 to 5
Northwest corner Loomis & Pickard (M-20), 5 miles east of Mt. Pleasant. 5 dealers

5 Ditman Shoes & Antiques
133 East Broadway
Mt. Pleasant , MI 48858
517 773-4652
By chance or appointment.
Downtown, north side of street.

6 Our Vintage Shop
620 South Mission (Business 27)
Mt. Pleasant , MI 48858
517 773-5116
Mon 11 to 4, Tues. to Sat. 10 to 5:30, Sun. by chance.
West side of highway, across road from Ric's Supermarket.

7 Valley Resale
Old 27 and River Rd
Mt Pleasant , MI 48858
517 772-5268
Mon. to Fri 10:30 to 5:30; Sat. by chance, but usually open.
South side of River Road just east of Old 27, 1 mile north of Mt. Pleasant.
Glass, pottery, antiques and used furniture.

MOUNT PLEASANT DETAIL MAP

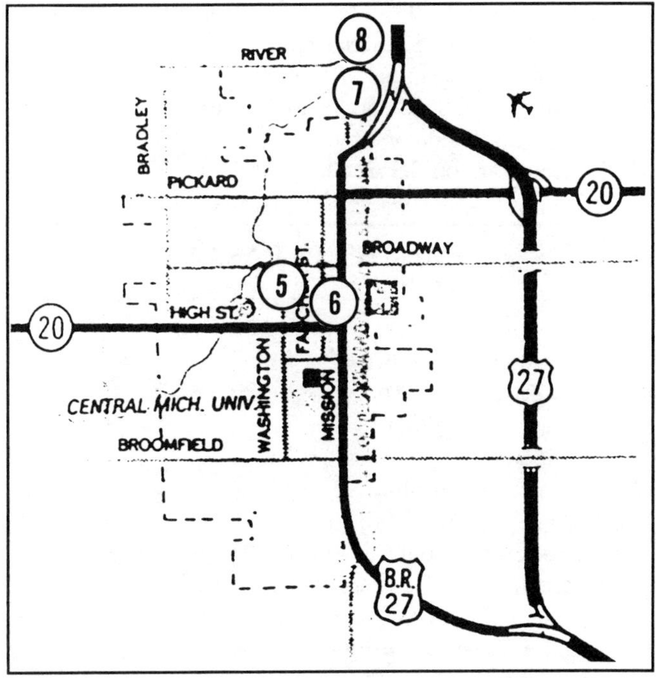

8 Riverside Antiques & Collectibles
993 S Mission Road
Mt Pleasant , MI 48858
517 773-3946
Mon. to Sat. 11 to 5; Sun. by chance.
North on Old 27, east side of road just north of river.
Dried flowers, candles, primitives, collectibles and gifts.

WEIDMAN

9 Chippewa Bend Antiques & Collectibles
650 North School Street
Weidman, MI 48893
517 644-5398
By chance or appointment.
Glassware, etc.

TIER 7
THE U.S. 10 ROUTE

7.1 MASON COUNTY

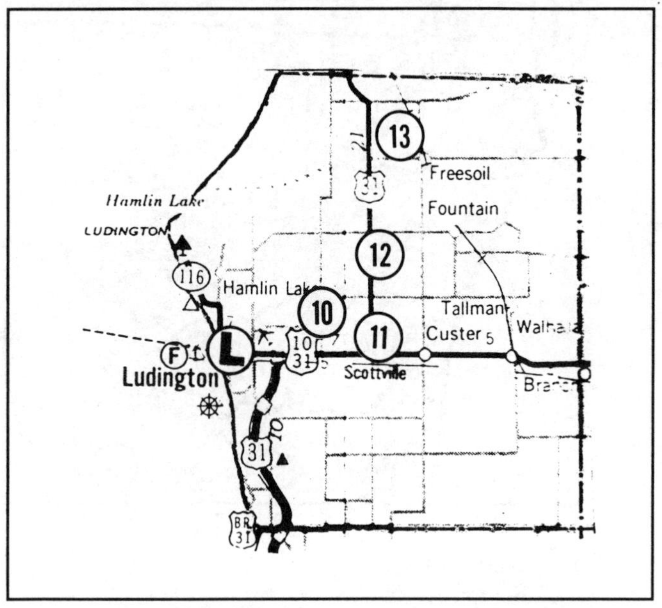

L: 1 to 9 - Ludington, see Detail Map

Recommended Points of Interest:
* Rose Hawley Museum, 115 W. Loomis, 616 843-2001
* White Pine Village, 1687 S. Lakeshore, 616 843-4808

For Additional Information:
* Mason County Visitors Bureau, 616 845-0324

LUDINGTON

1 Sandpiper Emporium
809 West Ludington Avenue
Ludington , MI 49431
616 843-3008
Summer: Mon. to Sat. 9 a.m. to 9 p.m., Sun. 10 to 5
Winter: Mon. to Sat. 9:30 to 5:30, Sun. 12 to 4
Southeast corner Lakeshore Drive & Ludington Avenue.
Antiques as part of gift & apparel shop in resort complex.

7.1 Mason County - continued

LUDINGTON DETAIL MAP

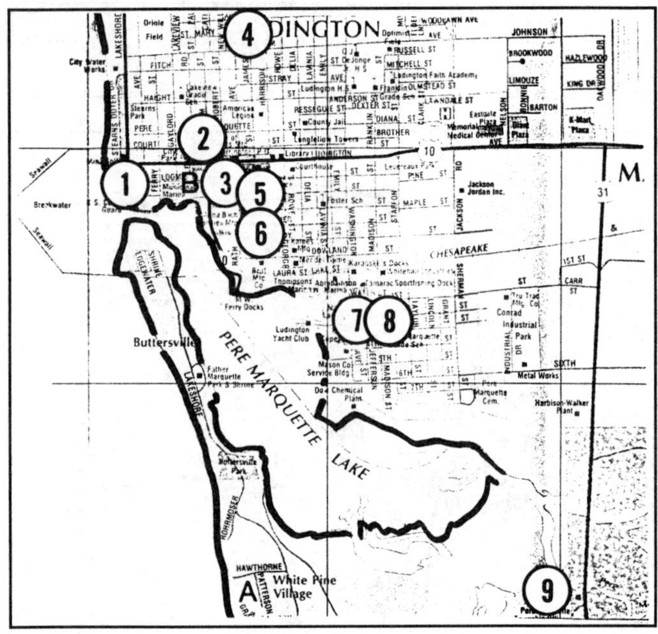

2 Cole's Antiques Villa
322 W. Ludington Avenue
Ludington , MI 49431
616 845-7414
Weekends, Spring and Fall; Daily May thru Aug. & Dec. D
Closed January & February.
West end of downtown, just east of the House of Flavors.

3 Country Charm
119 West Ludington Avenue
Ludington , MI 49431
616 843-4722
Summer: Mon. to Sat. 10 to 8; also Sun. 12 to 4 July & Aug. Winter: Thurs. to Sat. 11 to 5
Downtown
Antique shop plus gift shop.

4 Garden Path Interiors
1011 North James Street
Ludington , MI 49431
616 845-5353; FAX: 616 845-1410
Mon. to Sat. 9 to 6
Corner of James Street & Bryont Road.
Antiques, gifts, decorative accessories

5 The Antique Store
127 South James
Ludington , MI 49431
616 845-5888; (708 852-8170 off season)
May to mid-Oct.: Mon. to Sat. 11 to 5;
Downtown, one block south of Ludington Street, northeast corner James & Loomis.

6 Granny's Attic Antiques & Collectibles
325 South James Street
Ludington , MI 49431
616 843-4477
June to Labor Day: Mon. to Fri. 11 to 4, Sat. 11 to 3
Downtown, northeast corner Foster & James.

7 Washington Antiques
1001 South Washington Avenue
Ludington , MI 49431
616 843-8030
Mon. to Sat. 10 to 5
Southeast corner 2nd & Washington. Lots of furniture.

8 Christa's Antiques & Collectibles
1002 South Madison
Ludington , MI 49431
616 845-0075
April to Oct.: Mon. to Sat. 10 to 5;
Nov. to March: Fri. & Sat. 10 to 5
SWC 2nd & Madison, 10 blocks south of U.S. 10.

9 Frontier Corner Antiques
5590 Iris Road & Old 27
Ludington , MI 49431
616 843-8567
April 1 to Dec. 31: Every day 11 to 5
Just west of Old 27, in back of Zephyr Gas Station.

10 Always Antique Mall
2144 Johnson Road
Ludington, MI 49431
616 843-8781
Summer: Every day 11 to 5;
Winter: Fri. to Sun. 11 to 5; closed Jan.
Midway between Ludington and Scottsville go north on Styles Street 1/4 mile to Johnson Road, then east 1/4 mile; north side of road. Opened 1994

SCOTTVILLE

11 Frick's Old Country Store
120 North Main Street
Scottville , MI 49454
616 757-4708
By chance, summer only.
Downtown, southeast corner Broadway & North Main

12 School House Antiques
2872 N. U.S. 31
Scottville , MI 49454
616 757-9364
Open every day 10 to 5
NEC Sugar Grove & U.S. 31, 3 miles north of Scottville.
Primitives, country, windmills, etc.

FREE SOIL

13 Country Style Antiques
6601 Stephens Road
Free Soil , MI 49411
616 462-3706
Thurs. to Sat. 11 to 5
East from U.S. 31 on Fountain Road 4 miles to Stevens; north on Stevens.

WALHALLA

14 Knotty Pine Antique Mall
6796 East U.S. 10
Walhalla , MI 49458
616 757-9426
Thurs. to Sat. 10 to 5, Sun. 11 to 5
North side of the highway at the curve, 22 miles east of Ludington.
23 dealers

7.2 LAKE COUNTY

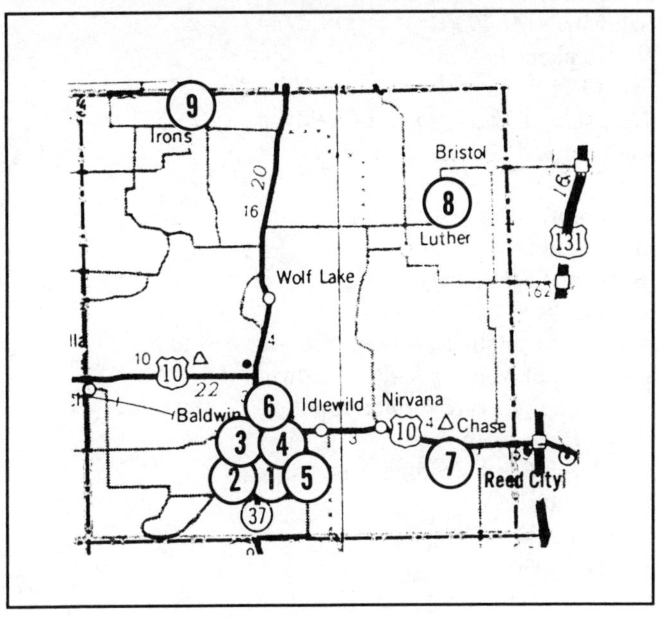

Recommended Points of Interest:

* Shrine of the Pines, Baldwin, 616 745-7892

For Additional Information:

* Lake County Chamber of Commerce, 616 745-4331

BALDWIN

1 Star Sales House
M-37, 3 mi. S. of Baldwin
Baldwin , MI 49304
616 745-3612
May 1 to Nov 1: Thurs. to Mon. 10 to 5, Sun. 10 to 3.
SEC M-37 & Star Lake Road, 3 miles south of Baldwin.
Furniture, primitives, glass, etc. Nice shop in rustic house.

2 Paul Bunyan Antiques Mall
3252 South M-37
Baldwin , MI 49304
616 745-2637
Daily Mid-March to Mid-Nov. Evenings and winter weekends by chance or appointment.
3 miles south of Baldwin, west side of highway.

3 Shirley & Pat's Collectibles Antiques
M-37 South
Baldwin , MI 49304
No telephone listed.
Fri. 12 to 5; Sat. 10 to 5; Sun. 10 to 2
West side of M-37, south of Baldwin
Antiques and household goods.

4 Painted Pony Antiques
M-37 South
Baldwin , MI 49304
616 745-7440
April 1 to Christmas: Thurs. thru Mon. 10 to 5
West side of M-37, south of Baldwin.
Small shop; glass & furniture, pottery, jewelry, etc.

5 River Bend Trading Post
M-37 South
Baldwin , MI 49304
616 745-4030
May 1 to Dec.: Every Day 10 to 6
Northeast corner M-37 & Carroll's Trail
Country, primitive, glass, smalls.

6 Touch of Yesteryear
767 Michigan Avenue (Main Street)
Baldwin , MI 49304
616 745-7877
April through Dec.: Fri to Sun. 10 to 5:30; other times by chance.
Downtown

CHASE

7 A & A Chase Country Store
100 Main Street
Chase , MI 49623
616 832-3356
May to Nov.: Sat. 9 to 6; Sun. & Mon. 10 to 6; other hours by appointment.
On U.S. 10
"Antiques, collectibles & junque."

LUTHER

8 Hopeful Antiques
Skookum Road
Luther , MI 49656
616-829-3977
Daily 10 to 5
Midway between Luther and Bristol, 10 miles west of U.S. 131.
Outstanding collection of glass, pottery, lamps, primitives & decoys.

9 Wheeler Dealer Store
10 1/2 Mile Road
Irons , MI 49644
616 266-5521
Mon. to Sat. 8 to 5, Sun. 9 to 3
Downtown, at the lumber yard, south side of road.
The Haggle Hut is just down the street.

MAP OF OSCEOLA COUNTY:

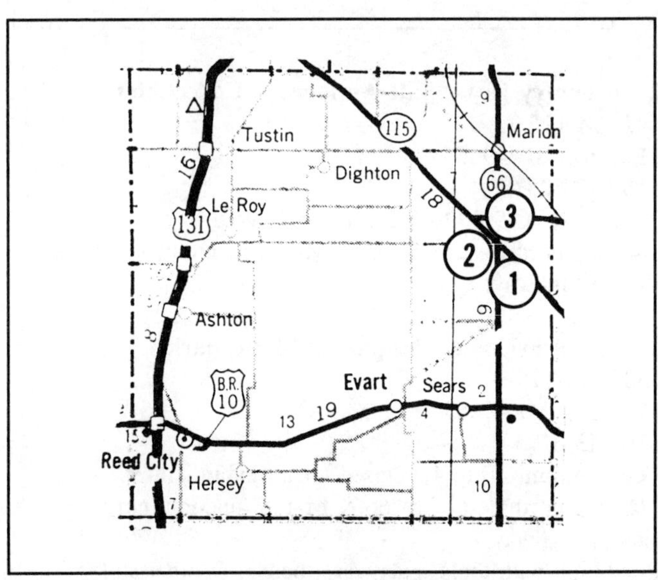

7.3 OSCEOLA

(Map on preceding page.)

For Additional Information:
* Evart Chamber of Commerce, 616 734-5555

EVART

1 LC's Chicken Coop
1014 North M-66
Evart , MI 49631
616 743-2456
By chance or appointment
2 1/2 miles south of M-115, east side of road between 12 & 13 Mile Roads.
Small blue shed near the house.

MARION

2 Country Heart Side Antiques & Collectibles
4421 M-115
Marion , MI 49665
616 743-6287
April to Nov. 9:30 to 5 Daily except Wed.
1/4 mile northwest of M-66 & M-115 junction, southwest side of highway.

3 Good Friend's Antiques and Flea Market
15396 M-115
Marion , MI 49665
616 743-6173
Tues. to Sun. 10 to 4; closed for a time in winter.
1/4 mile northwest of M-66 & M-115 junction, northeast side of highway.
Piled high with tools, glassware, books, & other stuff.

7.4 CLARE COUNTY

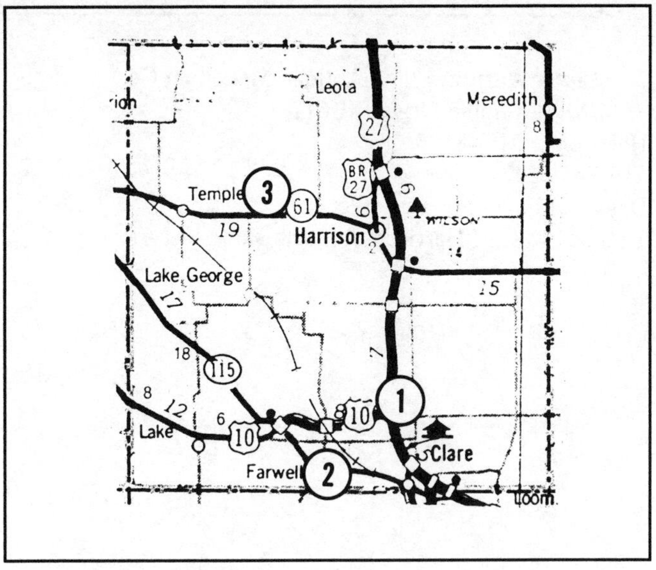

For Additional Information:
* Clare Chamber of Commerce, 517 386-2442

CLARE

1 House of Antiques & Collectibles
10472 South Clare Avenue (Old U.S. 27)
Clare, MI 48617
517 386-3571
Open daily.
North of Clare, west side of highway.
Glassware, dolls, etc.

FARWELL

2 Main Street Market Place
175 West Main Street
Farwell , MI 48622
517 588-4466
Mon. to Fri. 11 to 6, closed Thurs.; Sun. 12 to 5
Downtown Farwell, 5 miles west of Clare.

HARRISON

3 **Lott's Antiques** (aka Antique Marketing Co.)
7112 West Temple Drive (M-61)
Harrison , MI 48625
616 743-6222
Days and hours not available.
10 miles west of Harrison on north side of M-61.

MAP OF MANISTEE COUNTY:

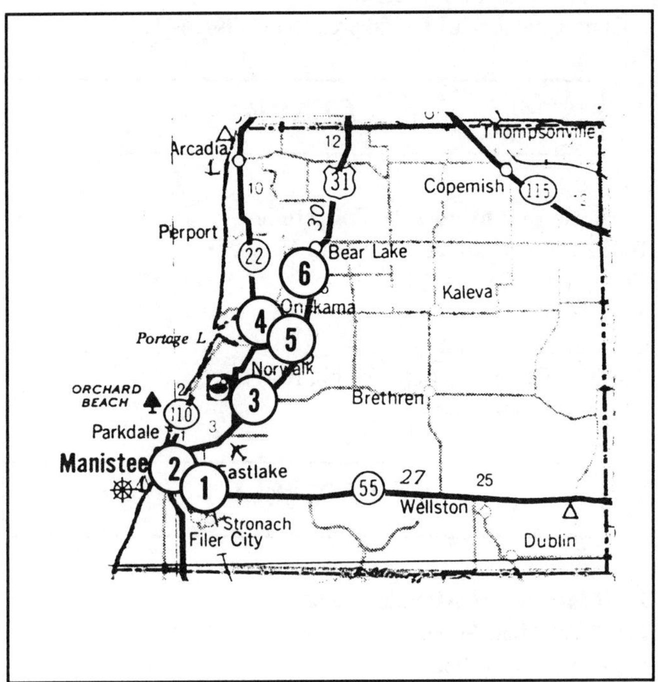

TIER 8
THE M-55 ROUTE

8.1 MANISTEE COUNTY

(Map on preceding page.)

Recommended Points of Interest:
* Old Manistee Waterworks Museum, 616 723-5331

For Additional Information:
* Manistee County Chamber of Commerce, 616 723-2575

MANISTEE

1 Sawduster's Crafts & Collectibles Antique Mall
362 First Street
Manistee , MI 49660
616 723-0130
Tues. to Sun. 12 to 6
Northeast corner First & Greenbush, just south of downtown.
Smalls, very little furniture.

2 Diana & Co.
294 River Street
Manistee , MI 49660
616 723-2881
Mon. to Sat. 10 to 5, Sun. 1 to 4
Downtown, north side of street.

3 North Country Antiques
Chippewa (U.S. 31)
Manistee , MI 49660
616 723-5675
Open all year by chance or appointment.
7 miles north of Manistee, house on west side of highway.

ONEKAMA

4 The Old Farm Store
8011 First Street
Onekama , MI 49675
616 889-3733
Memorial Day to Oct. 15: Mon. to Sat. 10 to 4.
Northeast corner M-22 & 8 Mile Road, south end of town, 1 1/4 mile west of U.S. 31.

5 Jack Burchard Antiques
5119 Main Street
Onekama , MI 49675
616 889-4451
By chance.
Downtown, across from the Pizza King.

BEAR LAKE

6 Bear Lake Antique Mall
11590 Chippewa Highway (U.S. 31)
Bear Lake , MI 49614
616 864-2327
Summer: Mon. & Thurs. to Sat. 10 to 6, Sun. 12 to 5
15 mi. N. of Manistee on west side of US 31, across from golf course.

See the notice about Antique Trek on the inside back cover. Come to the southwest corner of Michigan Veterans Day Weekend for antique related lectures, workshops, special events, and a major antique auction.

8.2 WEXFORD COUNTY

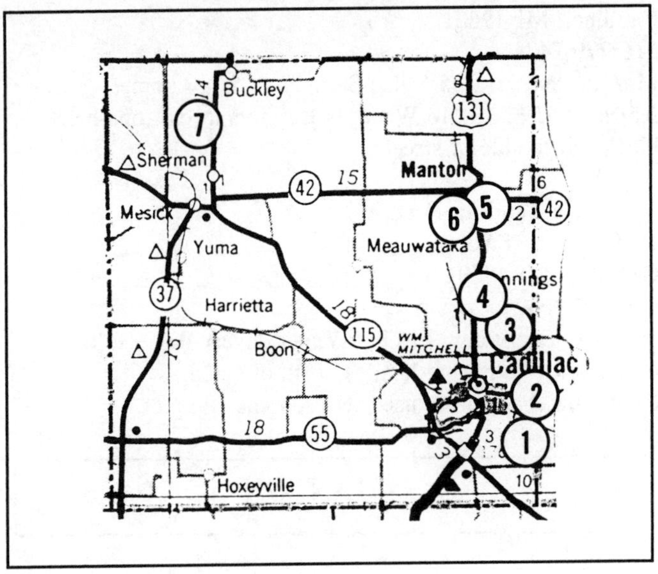

Recommended Points of Interest:
* Wexford County Historical Museum, 616 775-1717

For Additional Information:
* Cadillac Chamber of Commerce, 616 775-9776

CADILLAC

1 Phyllis' Olde House Antiques
7803 South 45 Mile Road
Cadillac , MI 49601
616 775-7502
Sun. to Fri. by chance or appointment.
East 2 miles from US 131 on Paluster Road (where M-55 turns west), around the bend; on the east side of the road. Shop in home, with glassware, plates, smalls.

2 Scholten's Antiques
10600 East Division
Cadillac , MI 49601
616 775-7504 Open any time.
2 miles east of Cadillac on M-55 at Hemlock Drive.
House on south side of highway. Furniture, pottery, etc.

3 Royer's Antiques
311 Bell
Cadillac, MI 49601
616 779-2434
Mon. to Sat. 10 to 5; also Sun. 12 to 5 in summer.
North on U.S. 131 to Wendy's Restaurant, east one-half block, north side of street.

4 Steve's Trading Post
1989 U.S. 131 South
Cadillac, MI 49601
616 775-3057
Summer: Every day 9 to 8; Winter: Every day 9 to 6
East side of highway, 3 miles north of Cadillac.
Crafts, baseball cards, used items, some antiques.

MANTON

5 Antiques Unique
407 North Michigan (U.S. 131)
Manton, MI 49663
616 824-3852
Mon. to Sat. 10:30 to 5, Sun. 11 to 5, closed Wed.
West side of street. Dolls & doll repair, etc.

6 Manton Antiques
212 S Michigan (U.S. 131)
Manton , MI 49663
616 824-3783
Mon. to Sat. 9 to 5; Sun. 1 to 5
NWC Williams Street, 2 blocks south of downtown.
Furniture; collectible teddy bears; hardware; toy trains.

MESICK

7 Hide-away Antiques and Sugar Bush
9431 N 13 Mile (M-37)
Mesick , MI 48668
616 269-3473
Open all year by chance or appointment.
Mid-way between Sherman and Buckley.
Primitives and collectibles

8.3 MISSAUKEE COUNTY

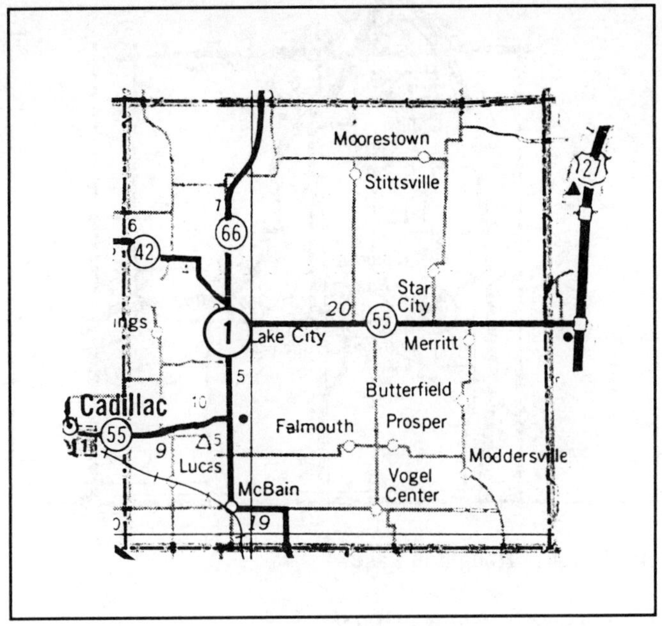

LAKE CITY

1 Sue's Treasure Trove
433 S Lake Shore Dr
Lake City , MI 49651
616 839-2145
Spring to Fall: 11 to 5 by chance or appointment.
Home on residential street, across from the lake.

8.4 ROSCOMMON COUNTY

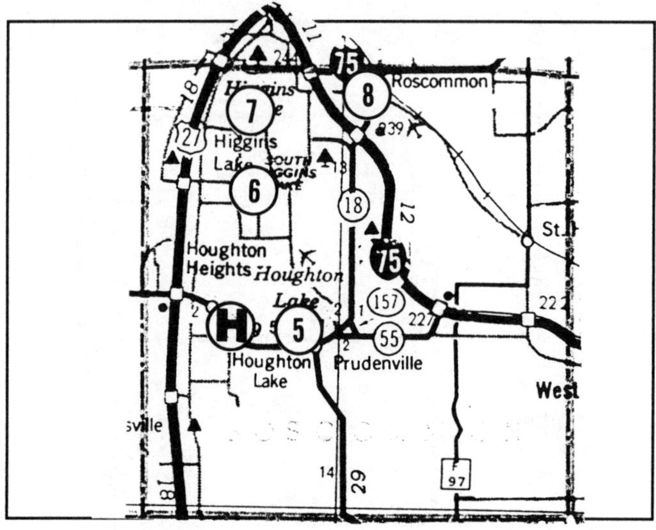

H: 1 to 4 - Houghton Lake

Recommended Points of Interest:
* Civilian Conservation Corps Museum, North Higgins Lake State Park, 517 821-6125

For Additional Information:
* Houghton Lake Chamber of Commerce, 517 366-5644

HOUGHTON LAKE

1 Rose Arbor Antiques
105 Lake (Knapp Road) Zone 7
Houghton Lake, MI 48629
517 422-4805
April to Dec.: Mon. to Sat. 10 to 5, Sun. 12 to 4
3 miles east of U.S. 27.

2 Berta's Antiques
5800 West Houghton Lake Drive
Houghton Lake, MI 48629
517 422-4104
Summer: Thurs. to Mon. 11 to 5; Winter: Fri. 11 to 5, Sat. 11 to 5, Sun. 1 to 5, Mon. & Tues. by appointment.
North side of road a half mile west of Loxley Road.

3 Houghton Lake Flea Market
1499 Loxley Road
Houghton Lake, MI 48629
517 422-3011; 517 422-5396
Every Day: 8 to 4, year-round.
East side of road, just south of School Road.
Not a flea market: a large 10,000 square foot quality antique shop.

4 Maxine's Antiques
7810 School Road
Houghton Lake, MI 48629
517 422-5751
Summer (April to Dec.): Mon. to Sat. 9 to 4;
Winter: By chance
From Old 27 east on M-55 1.4 miles to Loxley Road, then south .5 mile to School Road, then east .2 mile; south side of road.
Good quality furniture.

PRUDENVILLE

5 The Carousel Shoppe
1460 West Houghton Lake Drive
Prudenville, MI 48651
517 366-5477
Open Summer only.
West side of town, NWC Iroquois & Houghton Lake Drive.

HIGGINS LAKE

6 Yorty's Antiques
103 Yorty Drive (West Higgins Lake Drive)
Higgins Lake, MI 48627
517 821-9242
Summer
Just east of the U.S. 27 interchange, at Old 27 & Pine Drive (County Road 104), there is a large sign pointing the way to local business establishments. From here go east on Pine Road 1.8 miles to Hillcrest Road, then north 1.7 miles to West Higgins Lake Drive, then east 1.4 miles. North side of road, across from Higgins Lake Food Market.

7 Farley's Antique Treasure Trove
10028 West Higgins Lake Drive
Higgins Lake, MI 48627
517 821-6478
Memorial Day to Labor Day: Wed. to Sat. 12 to 6, Sun. 12 to 4
From U.S. 27: Higgins Lake exit east to Old 27, then north 6 miles. Look for the sign at Haines Street pointing the way to local business establishments. Go east one block, then north one block on West Higgins Lake Road; east side of street. (Follow signs.)
A shop called Ginger's Collectibles is next door to the north.

ROSCOMMON

8 T.J.'s Oldies & Goodies
821 Lake Street
Roscommon, MI 48653
517 275-5321
April to Oct.: Mon. to Sat. 10 to 5;
Feb. & March: Wed. to Sat. 10 to 5; closed Jan.
Downtown, just north of tracks, west side of street.

TIER 9
THE M-72 ROUTE

9.1 BENZIE COUNTY

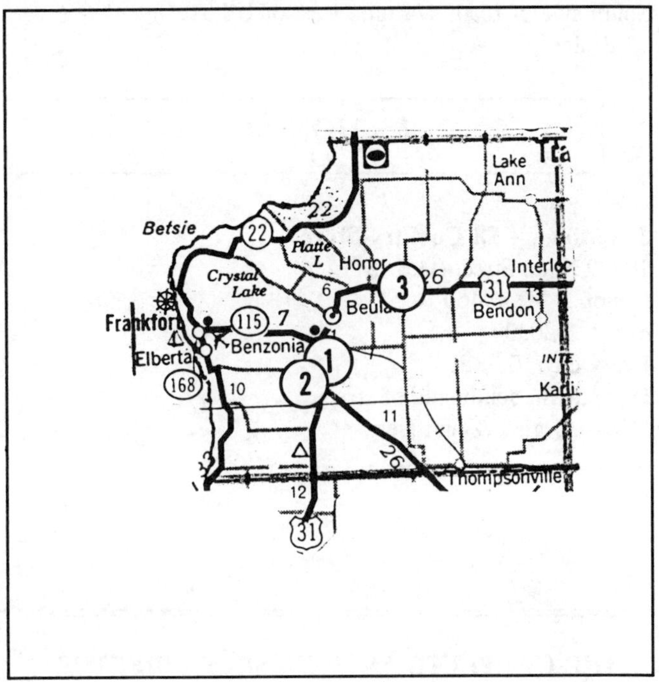

Recommended Points of Interest:
* Gwen Frostic Prints Studio, Benzonia, 616 882-5505

For Additional Information:
* Benzie County Chamber of Commerce, 616 882-5802

BENZONIA

1 Benzonia Antique Mall
M-115 & US 31
Benzonia , MI 49616
616 882-7063
Summer: Every Day 10 to 5;
Winter: Thurs. to Sat. 10 to 5; closed Feb.
2 mi. south of Benzonia, east side U.S.31 south of M-115.

2 Archy's Antiques & Treasure House
M-115 East
Benzonia , MI 49616
616 882-7232
Summer: Wed. to Mon. 10 to 5; Winter: Thurs. to Mon. 11 to 5
South side of road, 1/4 mile west of US 31.
12 dealers.

HONOR

3 Money's Ol Country Store
10929 Main Street (U.S. 31)
Honor , MI 49460
616 325-2030
Every day 10 to 5.
Downtown, south side of street.
"Unusual gifts & antiques."

9.2 LEELANAU COUNTY

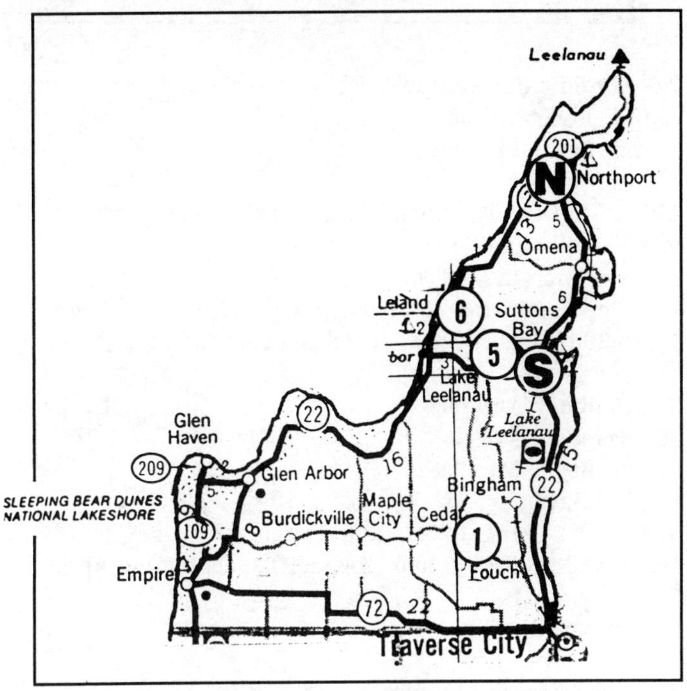

S: 2 to 4 - Suttons Bay
N: 6 to 14 - Northport

Recommended Points of Interest:
* Sleeping Bear Dunes National Lakeshore

For Additional Information:
* Leelanau County Chamber of Commerce, 616 256-9801

FOUCH (TRAVERSE CITY)

1 Georgia & Les Plantz Antiques
6881 East Fouch Road (#614)
Traverse City , MI 49684
616 947-7919
Mon. to Sat. by chance or appointment.
North on M-22 to Cherry Bend Road (633), west 3 miles on Cherry Bend Road to County Road 614, west three miles, north side of road.
No furniture.

SUTTONS BAY

2 Sutton's Bay Galleries
224 St. Joseph Avenue
Suttons Bay , MI 49682
616 271-4444
May 15 to Dec. 31: Mon. to Sat. 10:30 to 5:30; Sun. 12 to 4;
Jan. 1 to May 15 by chance.
Downtown, southeast corner St. Joseph & Jefferson Streets.
16th - 20th Century Fine Art and Antiquarian Prints.

3 Danbury Antiques
305 St Joseph Avenue
Suttons Bay , MI 49682
616 271-3211
May to Oct.: Mon. to Sat. 10 to 6; Sun. 12 to 4;
Dec.: Wed. to Sat. 10 to 6; Closed Oct. and Jan. to April.
Downtown
English smalls.

4 Architectural Antiques
301 St. Joseph Avenue
Suttons Bay , MI 49682
616 271-6821
Summer: Mon. to Sat. 9:30 to 5;
Winter: Tues. to Sat. 9:30 to 5.
Downtown

LAKE LEELANAU

5 Provemont General Store
102 Meinard Street,
Lake Leelanau , MI 49653
616 256-9954
Mon. to Sat. 10 to 5; Sun. 12 to 5, or by appointment.
Downtown
General line; Americana; tools; glass; linens; collectibles.

LELAND

6 The Old Library
103 East River Street
Leland , MI 49654
616 256-7428; 616 256-9119
Summer: Mon. to Sat. 10 to 6; Sun. 12 to 5;
Winter: By chance.
Downtown, across from historic Bluebird Restaurant.

NORTHPORT

7 Grandma's Trunk
102 Mill Street
Northport , MI 49670
616 386-5351
May 1 to Labor Day: 10 to 6 every day;
Labor Day to Christmas: 10 to 5 every day.

8 Fifth Street Antiques
211 East 5th Street
Northport , MI 49670
616 386-5421
Daily during season.

9 Cobweb Treasures
393 West Street
Northport , MI 49670
616 386-5532
Mid-June to Mid-Oct.: Daily 10 to 6;
Winter by appointment or chance.
South side of town, 1 block west of M-22/201 light, east side of street.

10 Willowbrook Antiques
201 North Mill Street
Northport , MI 49670
616 387-5617
Summer: Every day 8 to 10.
Downtown

11 Heathman Antiques & Finery
210 Mill Street
Northport , MI 49670
616 386-7007
July & Aug.: Tues. to Sat. 10 to 5
Downtown, east side of street.
Antiques, reproductions, new decorative items.

12 Bird-n-Hand
12271 East Woolsey Lake (Co. Road 640)
Northport , MI 49670
616 386-7104
May to Dec.: call for hours.
2 miles north of Northport.
Hand crafted gifts, wreaths, and antiques.

13 Birdcage Antiques
118 W. Main
Northport, MI 49670
616 386-5482 (answering machine)
Days and hours not available.

14 Back Roads Antiques
116 East Nagonaba
Northport, MI 49670
616 386-7011
Wed. to Sat.: 10 to 6; Sun.: 12 to 6;
Mon. & Tues. by chance or appointment
Near the marina.
Antiques, collectibles, local folkart.

9.3 GRAND TRAVERSE COUNTY

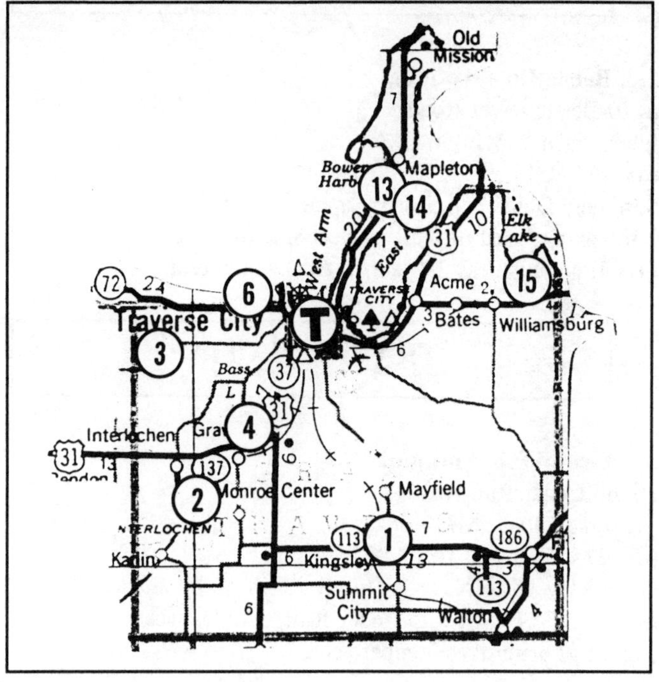

T: 7 TO 12 - Traverse City, see Detail Map

Recommended Points of Interest:
* Con Foster Museum, Traverse City, 616 922-4905

For Additional Information:
* Grand Traverse Visitors Bureau, 616 947-1120

KINGSLEY

1 B & E Antiques
260 E. Main (M-113)
Kingsley, MI 49649
616 263-7677
Tues. to Sat. 10 to 5, Sun. 12 to 5
Just east of downtown, south side of the street.
Antiques, collectibles, sports cards, etc.

INTERLOCHEN

2 Betsie-Bo's Antiques
6470 Betsie River Road
Interlochen , MI 49643
616 276-9514
Summer: Daily 1 to 5 or by appointment.
2 miles northeast of Karlin, west side of road.
In antique business 25 years. Also canoe rental.

TRAVERSE CITY

3 Grey Wolf Antiques
20766 Cedar Run Road
Traverse City , MI 49684
616 275-7471 or 616 620-3158
Open May 15 to Nov. 1; 9 to 8. Winter: by chance.
West on Front Street to Cedar Run, 9 miles west.
Lighting, primitives, copper, etc.

4 Chum's Corner Antique Mall
4200 US 31 South
Traverse City , MI 49684
616 943-4200
Daily 10 to 6 year round.
North side of U.S. 31, 1/4 mile west of M-37.

5 Antique Emporium
565 Blue Star Drive
Traverse City , MI 49684
616 943-3658
Daily 10 to 6; (Open to 8 Fri. & Sat. June to Sept.)
Northeast corner Blue Star Drive & US 31, 1 1/2 miles north of Chums Corner. 4,000 square feet.

6 Devonshire Antiques
5085 Barney Rd
Traverse City , MI 49684
616 947-1063
Open April thru December: Thurs. thru Sat. 11 to 5.
July & August: Tues. thru Sat. 11 to 5.
W. Front to Cedar Run to Barney Road; south side of road.

TRAVERSE CITY DETAIL MAP

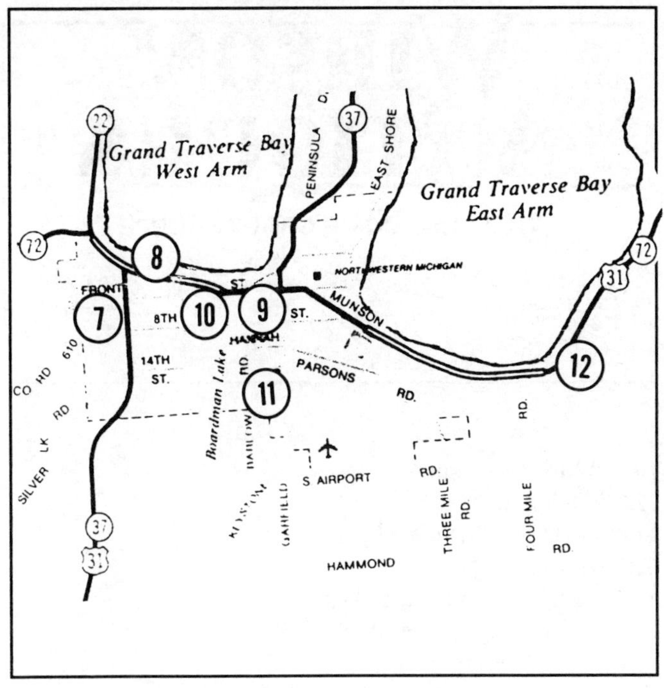

7 Custer Antiques
826 West Front Street
Traverse City , MI 49684
616 929-9201
Open year round; hours vary, call ahead.
Northeast corner Spruce Street, west of downtown.

8 Antique Company - West
221 Grand View Parkway
Traverse City , MI 49684
616-947-3211
Every day 10 to 6
Across from the power plant, 1/2 block east of Union.
25 dealers. Lots of stuff.

9 Antiques & Art
544 East Eighth Street
Traverse City , MI 49684
616 946-0424
Mon. to Sat. 12 to 5
Parking in back of the small shop; turn south on Franklin Street.

10 Wilson Antiques
123 S Union St
Traverse City , MI 49684
616 946-4177
Mon. to Sat. 10 to 6; Sun. 11 to 5
Downtown; free parking off State Street.
50 dealers, 4 floors.

11 Rickman's Antiques
628 Fern Street
Traverse City , MI 49684
616 946-6609
Mon. to Fri. 10 to 6; Sat. 12 to 5
Off the beaten path. Find the corner of Fern and Eighth Street; Fern is the next street west of Garfield. Go south on Fern from Eighth 2 1/2 blocks to the railroad tracks (Fern is unpaved part of the way). The shop is down a long driveway to the west.
Lots of refinished oak and other furniture. 8,000 square feet.

12 Antique Company - East
4386 US 31 North
Traverse City , MI 49684
616 938-3000
Summer: Every day 10 to 6;
Jan. to March (or April): Fri. to Sun. 10 to 6
East side of town, east of Holiday, across the highway from the Bay in back of Troutman, just north of the Traverse Bay Woolen Company.

13 Cherry Acres Antiques
12396 Peninsula Drive
Traverse City , MI 49484
616 223-4813
Mon. to Sat. 10 to 5, Sun. by chance.
8 miles north on Peninsula Drive.
Advertising, furniture, tins, postcards, old toys, and collectibles.

14 Walt's Antiques
2513 Nelson Rd
Traverse City , MI 49684
616 223-7386; or 616 223-4123
Open year round - hours vary off season.
8 miles out M-37 on Old Mission Peninsula west on Nelson Road.
Antique gas pumps, globes, signs & other gas station memorabilia; all types of older Michigan license plates and slot machines.

WILLIAMSBURG

15 Bunk House Antiques
M-72
Williamsburg , MI 49690
616 267-5622 or 313 792-9692
May 15 to Oct. 15: Every day 10 to 5; Oct. to Dec.: By appointment.
North side of highway, one mile east of Williamsburg.
Country, primitives, etc.

9.4 KALKASKA COUNTY

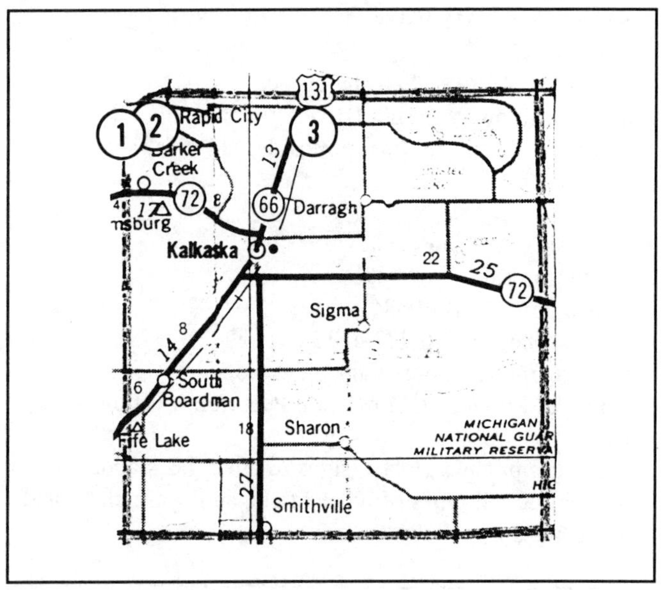

RAPID CITY

1 Miller's Antiques
Downtown Rapid City
Rapid City , MI 49676
616 331-6104
Summer: Daily 10 to 5; off season call first.
Downtown, southwest corner Harrison & Van Buren.

2 Kayle & Agnes Doty Antiques
6898 Crystal Beach Road
Rapid City , MI 49676
616 322-2807
Summer: Daily 10 to 4; Sunday by chance.
North side of road, 1 mile west of County Road 597.
Clocks & general line.

3 KG & Co.
7820 U.S. 131 N.E.
Mancelona, MI 49659
616 258-1100
Thurs. to Sun. 10 to 6, or by chance or appointment.
Between Mancelona & Kalkaska, south of Twin Lake Road.

9.5 CRAWFORD COUNTY

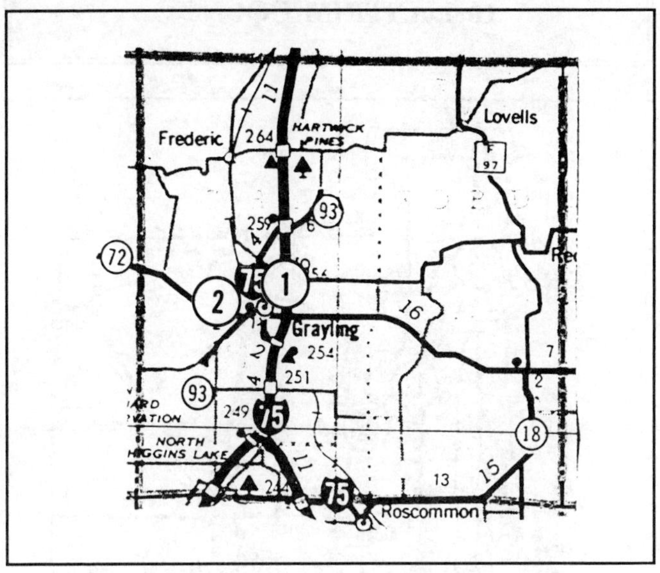

Recommended Points of Interest:

* Hartwick Pines Lumbering Museum, Hartwick Pines State Park, 517 348-7068

For Additional Information:

* Grayling Chamber of Commerce, 517 348-2921

GRAYLING

1 Potbelly Antiques
4729 North Down River Road
Grayling, MI 49738
517 348-8578
Apr. to Dec.: Daily 9 to 5; closed winters.
A mile east of Business I-75, south side of street in a grove of pine trees. Just west of I-75 Exit 256.

2 Ridley's Antiques
6930 M-72 West
Grayling, MI 49738
517 348-5907
March to Jan.: Every day 9 to 6
2 miles west of Grayling, north side of highway.

TIER 10
THE U.S. 31 ROUTE

10.1 ANTRIM COUNTY

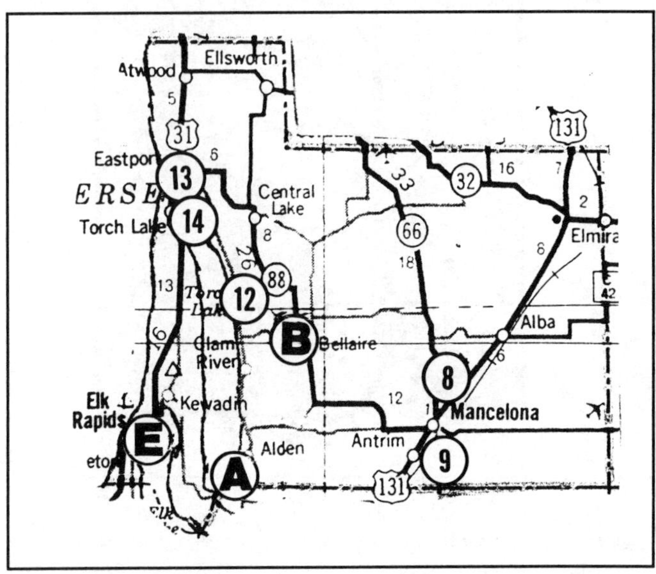

E: 1 to 3 - Elk Rapids
A: 4 to 7 - Alden
B: 9 to 11 - Bellaire

Recommended Points of Interest:
* Bellaire Historical Museum, 616 533-8943

For Additional Information:
* Elk Rapids Chamber of Commerce, 616 264-8202
* Bellaire Chamber of Commerce, 616 533-6023

ELK RAPIDS

1 A Summer Place Ltd.
125 River Street
Elk Rapids , MI 49629
616 264-6556; (off season: 517 631-0509)
Mem. to Labor Day: Mon. to Sat. 10 to 5, Sun. 12 to 4.
Spring & Fall by chance.
Downtown

2 Ginny's Emporium
145 River
Elk Rapids, MI 49629
616 264-8194

3 Joe's Antiques
101 Bridge Street
Elk Rapids , MI 49629
616 264-5199; 616 264-9976
May to Oct. 1.: Every Day 10 to 4
Downtown

ALDEN

4 Country Interiors & Antiques
9046 Helena
Alden , MI 49612
616 331-6188
Every day 10 to 5
Downtown.
Gifts, housewares, quilts, & antiques.

5 Antrim Antiques
9053 Helena Street
Alden , MI 49612
616 331-6468
May to Oct.: Sun. 12 to 5; Thur. 10 to 9; Other days 10 to 5
Downtown.
Quilts; painted furniture; hunting & fishing collectibles.

6 Nona's
Helena Street, across from Post Office, downtown.
Alden, MI 49612
No telephone at shop. (Call 616 331-6161 for information.)
May to Oct.: Every Day 11 to 4:30

7 Talponia Books Ltd.
10545 Helena Street
Alden, MI 49612
616 331-6324
Memorial Day to Labor Day 9 to sundown.
From Traverse City east on M-72 ten miles from Acme.
Turn left at the Alden-Rapit City Hwy. Follow to Alden,
on the southeast corner of Torch Lake.

MANCELONA

8 Dee's Antiques
301 South Maple
Mancelona , MI 49659
616 587-8121
Summer: Mon. & Wed. to Sat.: 10 to 5;
Winter: Mon. & Wed. to Sat.: 11 to 5; (Call first.)
1 block south of U.S. 131, east side of street.
Dolls, teddy bears, Victorian, etc.

9 Red Windmill Antiques
3775 Doerr Road
Mancelona , MI 49659
616 587-5121
April 1 to Sept. 1: Every day 10 to 5; or by appointment.
Northwest corner U.S. 131 & Doerr Road.

BELLAIRE

9 Village Habitat
213 North Bridge Street
Bellaire , MI 49615
616 533-8367
May 1 to Aug. 31: Tues. to Sat. 10 to 4
Downtown, west side of the street, across from the theater.

10 Wanifred Smith Antiques
408 North Bridge Street
Bellaire , MI 49615
616 377-7504
July 4 to Labor Day: Mon. to Sat. 1 to 4
East side of street, across the bridge from downtown.

11 Batterby Antiques
226 North Bridge Street
Bellaire , MI 49615
No telephone listed.
Open by chance. East side of street, north end of downtown.

10.1 Antrim County - continued

12 Pandora's Box
E. Intermediate Lake Dr. between Central Lake & Bellaire
Bellaire , MI 49615
616 533-8813
June to Aug.: Daily 10 to 5, Wed. by chance.

EASTPORT

13 The Hinter Haus Antique & Gift Shop
4819 U.S. 31
Eastport , MI 49627
616 599-2311
Memorial Day to Oct.: Daily 10 to 5, Sun. by chance.
1 block south of M-88, west side of highway.

TORCH LAKE

14 School House Antiques
U.S. 31 North
Torch Lake , MI 49627
616 599-2056
Mid-June to Sept.: 10 to 5 daily except Tuesday.

MAP OF OTSEGO COUNTY:

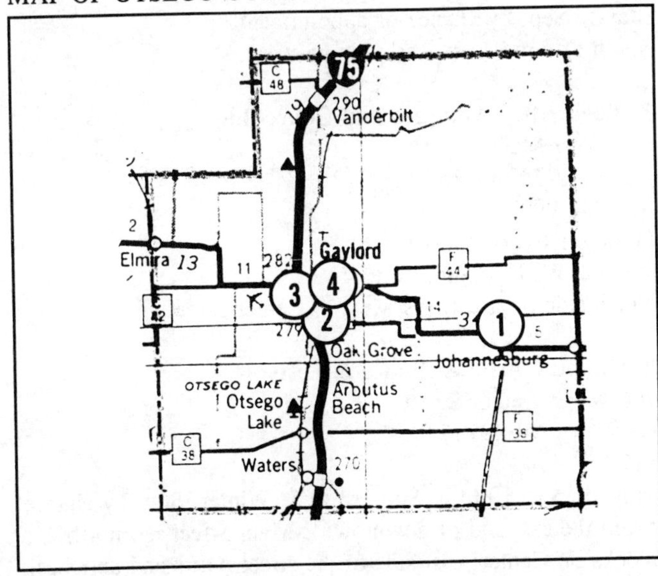

10.2 OTSEGO COUNTY

(Map on preceding page.)

For Additional Information:
* Gaylord Visitors Bureau, 517 732-4002

JOHANNESBURG

1 Cozy Corner Antiques
10816 M-32 East
Johannesburg, MI 49751
517 732-2225
Open Daily 9 to 6; Closed Wed.
NWC of intersection where M-32 turns south at light.

GAYLORD

2 The Castle
403 South Otsego
Gaylord, MI 49735
517 732-4665
May to Sep. by chance or appointment
South of downtown, east side of street.

3 Back Alley Antiques and Collectibles
110 West Main
Gaylord, MI 49735
517 732-8997
Summer: Every day 10 to 8;
Winter: Wed. to Sun. 10 to 4
North side of street, just west of Center Street.

4 Country Attic Antiques & Gifts
206 North Center Street
Gaylord, MI 49735
517 732-1142
Mon. to Sat. 10 to 6, Sun. 12 to 5; Winter: Sun. by chance.
From the east end of downtown's Main Street, go north 2 blocks on Center; east side of the street. Gifts and antiques.

10.3 CHARLEVOIX COUNTY

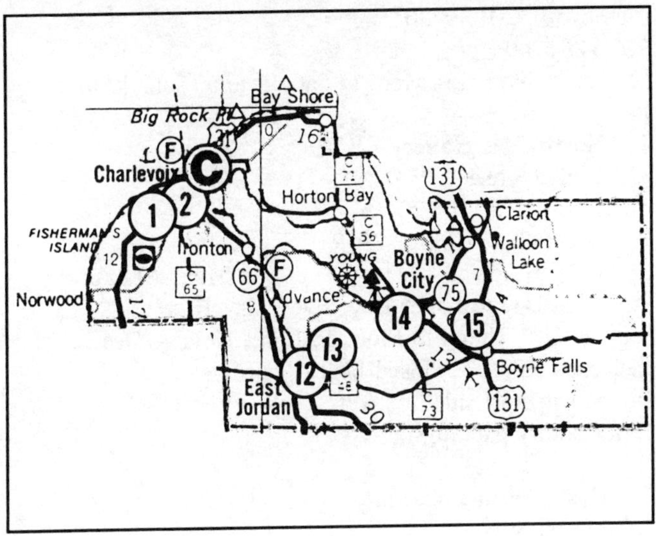

C: 3 to 11 - Charlevoix

Recommended Points of Interest:
* Earl Young Gnome Homes, Charlevoix

For Additional Information:
* Charlevoix Chamber of Commerce, 616 547-2102

CHARLEVOIX

1 The Sisters Antiques
U.S. 31 South
Charlevoix , MI 49720
616 547-6457; 616 547-6914
May 1 to Nov. 1: Mon. to Sat. 9:30 to 5:30; Sunday 1 to 5; or by appointment.
East side of highway, 2 miles south of Charlevoix.

2 Charlevoix Antique Mall
06522 U.S. 31 South
Charlevoix , MI 49720
616 547-5112
April to Dec.: Mon. to Sat. 10 to 5; Sun. 12 to 4 in season
1 mile south of Charlevoix. 20 dealers, 3,500 square feet.

3 The Garage Sale
555 Petoskey Avenue (U.S. 31 North)
Charlevoix, MI 49720
616 547-5700
May 15 to Nov. 15: Mon. to Sat. 10 to 5, Sun. 12 to 4

4 North Seas Gallery
330 Bridge Street
Charlevoix , MI 49720
616 547-0422; 616 547-2959
End of April to end of Dec.: Thurs. to Mon. 10 to 6;
Memorial Day to Labor Day: Every day 10 to 6;
Sept. & Oct. Thurs. to Mon. 10 to 6; Nov. & Dec.:
weekends only; Closed Jan. to April.
Downtown, east side of street.
19th Century paintings.

5 Rose Cottage Antiques
107 Mason Street
Charlevoix , MI 49720
616 547-0636, or 616 547-5842
Memorial Day to mid-Oct.: Wed. to Sat. 10 to 5, or by appointment.
Downtown, 1/2 block west of Bridge St. next to post office.

6 604 Bridge Antiques & Art
604 Bridge Street
Charlevoix, MI 49720
616 547-1273
Every Day 10 to 5
Northeast corner Bridge & Hurlbut Mission oak.

7 Shop of All Crafters
704 Bridge Street
Charlevoix , MI 49720
616 547-0257
Mid-May to Mid-Oct.: Every Day 10 to 6;
Winter: Fri. to Sun. 10 to 6
South of downtown. Mission oak.

8 Maison Jarin
228 Bridge Street
Charlevoix, MI 49720
616 547-0550
Summer: Every Day 10 to 5
Downtown

9 Kelly Antiques & Refinishing Co.
224 Stover Road
Charlevoix, MI 49720
616 547-9409
By Chance or Appointment: open most evenings & weekends.

10 Wooden Duck Antiques
03409 M-66
Charlevoix, MI 49720
616 547-5633
June 1 to Sept. 30: Tues. to Sat. 10 to 6
M-66 near Ironton Ferry
Specialize in antique decoys.

11 Stonehedge Galleries
5756 M-66
Charlevoix, MI 49720
616 547-5527
Mid-May to Mid-Oct.: Wed. to Sat. 19 to 5, Sun. 12 to 4
West side of highway, 1.5 miles south of Ironton Ferry.

EAST JORDAN

12 The Busy Bridge Antiques and Gifts
207 Main Street
East Jordan, MI 49727
616 536-3511
Mon. to Sat. 10 to 5:30; Sun. in July & Aug. 11 to 3
Downtown

13 Upstairs at the Bridge
Above the Busy Bridge
207 Main Street
East Jordan , MI 49727
616 536-3511
June to Dec.: Mon. to Sat. 10 to 5:30;
Sun. in July & Aug. 11 to 3
Second floor; entrance to the left of Busy Bridge shop.
8 dealers

BOYNE CITY

14 Apple-Bee Coterie Gifts & Antiques
111 N. Park Street
Boyne City , MI 49712
616 582-9208
May to Dec.: Mon. to Sat. 9:30 to 5;
Jan. to April: Fri. & Sat. only.
1 1/2 blocks north of downtown.
Gifts, antique linens & Glassware.

BOYNE FALLS

15 Boyne River Antiques
2030 U.S. 131
Boyne Falls , MI 49713
616 549-2344
May to Dec.: Mon. to Fri. 10 to 5, Sat. & Sun. 11 to 4;
Jan. to April: Fri. to Mon. 11 to 4
North of Boyne Falls.
Antiques, crafts, gifts, & art.

10.4 EMMET COUNTY

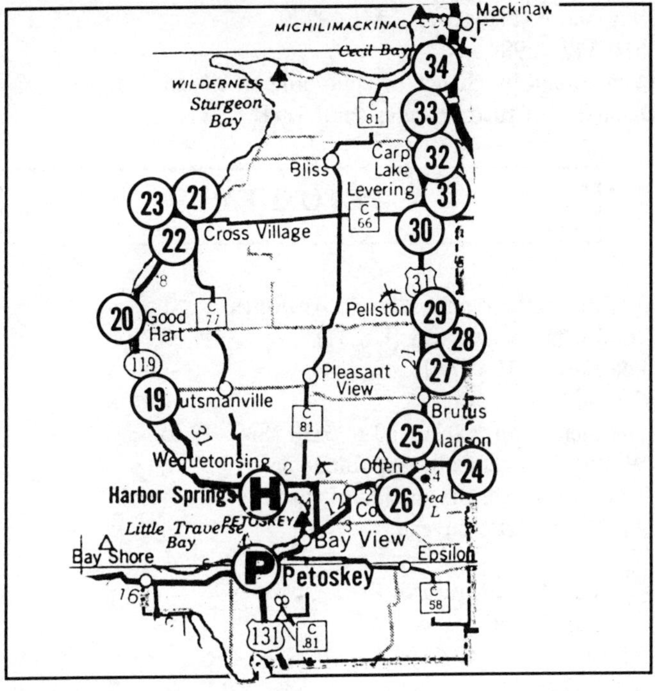

P: 3 to 11 - Petoskey
H: 13 to 18 - Harbor Springs

Recommended Points of Interest:
* Gaslight Historic District, downtown Petoskey
* Bay View, historic cottage community
* Rustic Legs Inn, Cross Village, 616 526-5381

For Additional Information:
* Petoskey Chamber of Commerce, 616 347-0200
* Harbor Springs Chamber of Commerce, 616 347-0200

BAY SHORE (PETOSKEY)

1 Glorie Be Gifts & Antiques
08591 Horton Bay Road
Bay Shore (Petoskey) , MI 49770
616 347-6759
Memorial Day to Oct.: Daily 10 to 5, Sun. 12 to 5.
West side of road, 2 miles south of U.S. 31.

2 Amish Way Antiques
08600 Camp Daggett Road
Bay Shore (Petoskey) , MI 49770
616 347-3898
Year-round by chance or appointment, closed Sun.
East side of road, 2 miles south of U.S. 31.

PETOSKEY

3 Joseph's World Classic Antiques
2680 Charlevoix Road (US 31)
Petoskey, MI 49770
616 347-0121
Summer: Mon. to Sat. 10 to 5:30, Sun. 12 to 4;
Winter: Weekends by appointment.
Two miles west, north side of road.
Art Deco, Art Nouveau.

4 Farr's Antiques & Etc.
331 Bay Street
Petoskey , MI 49770
616 347-0672
Mon. to Sat. 10:30 to 4:30, Sun. by chance.
Southeast corner Bay & Howard Streets.

5 Pettystuff
207 Howard
Petoskey , MI 49770
616 348-2627
Mon. to Sat. 10 to 5
Antique furniture and contemporary art.

6 Longton Hall Antiques
410 Rose Street
Petoskey , MI 49770
616 347-0672
Mon. to Sat. 1 to 5
In back of the parking lot for the Perry Hotel.

7 Marietta Antique Shop
106 East Mitchell Street (U.S. 31)
Petoskey , MI 49770
616 347-8369
Mon. to Sat. 10 to 5 SEC Mitchell & Elizabeth Streets.

8 For Love Not Money
314 East Lake Street
Petoskey, MI 49770
616 348-5533
Mon. to Sat. 10 to 5, Sun. 12 to 4
Downtown

9 Joie De Vie Antiques
1901 M-119 (Harbor-Petoskey Road)
Petoskey , MI 49770
616 347-1400; FAX 616 347-9029
Mem. to Labor Day: Mon. to Sat. 10 to 6, Sun. 11 to 5
Pink house across from Brown Motors, west side of the road.

10 The Blue Barn Antique Market
2022 M-119 (Harbor-Petoskey Road)
Petoskey , MI 49770
616 348-2022
Open all year; Mon. to Sat. 10 to 6; Sun. 12 to 4
East side of road, 3/4 mile north of U.S. 31.

11 Second Chance Furniture
2022 M-119
Petoskey , MI 49770
616 347-1131
Mon. to Fri. 9 to 5; Sat. 10 to 2
Located in back of Blue Barn Antique Market.

CONWAY

12 Desiree's Country Nostalgia
2343 Cook Avenue (West Conway Road)
Conway , MI 49722
616 347-8661
End of May to mid-Dec.: Sun. by chance.
North side of street, 1 block west of U.S. 31.

HARBOR SPRINGS

13 Huzza
136 Main Street East
Harbor Springs , MI 49740
616 526-2128
Summer: Mon. to Sat. 9:30 to 6; Winter 10 to 5; closed Mar. & April
Downtown, south side of street.
Antiques, interior design, home accessories.

14 Joie de Vie Antiques
138 East Main Street
Harbor Springs , MI 49740
616 526-7700
Memorial Day to Labor Day: Mon. to Sat. 10 to 6;
Winter: Mon. to Sat. 10 to 5
Downtown, south side of street.

15 Grant Interiors
8442 Harbor Petoskey Road (M-119 North)
Harbor Springs, MI 49770
616 347-8824
Mon. to Fri. 9 to 5, Sat. 9 to 2
In Harbor Plaza, south side of the highway, in front of the airport.

16 L'Esprit
195 West Main
Harbor Springs , MI 49740
616 526-9888
Mon. to Sat. 10 to 5.;
Also: July 4 to Labor Day: Sun. 12 to 3
SEC Main & Traverse, 2 blocks west of downtown.

17 Mauritshuis Antiques
345 East Main Street
Harbor Springs , MI 49740
616 526-7192; 616 526-5296
Mon. to Sat. 10 to 5
Just east of downtown, north side of street.
English and American furniture, paintings, and accessories.

18 Pooter Olooms Antiques
39 State
Harbor Springs , MI 49740
616 526-6101
June 1 to Labor Day: Mon. to Sat. 10 to 6; Sun. 11 to 4;
Winter: Mon. to Sat. 10 to 5, Sun. 11 to 3.
1.5 blocks north of Main, west side of street at curve.
Scandinavian country pine, quilts, folk art. 3,200 sq. ft.

19 TLC Summer Place
811 North Lakeshore (M-119)
Harbor Springs (Good Hart), MI 49740
616 526-7191; 616 526-7538
Summer: 7 Days 10 to 5;
Spring & Fall: Weekends 10 to 4
11 miles north of Harbor Springs.

GOOD HART

20 Good Hart Antiques
M-119
Good Hart , MI 49737
616 526-9533
Mon. to Sat. 10 to 5, or by appointment.
Next to the general store.

CROSS VILLAGE

21 The Red House at Cross Village
M-119 & State Road
Cross Village , MI 49723
616 526-2343
June 15 to Oct. 15: Every Day 10 to 5
M-119 & State Road
8 dealers.

22 Rose's Antiques & Collectibles
5550 N. Lakeshore Drive (M-119)
Cross Village, MI 49723
616 526-5934
April to Dec.: Usually every day 10 to 5:30.
1.5 miles south of Cross Village.

23 Lee's Dolls
Cross Village, MI 49723
616 526-7538
By appointment only.

ALANSON

24 Regina's Lakeview Antiques
M-68 West
Alanson, MI 49706
616 548-5398
May to Oct.: Mon. to Sat. 10 to 5, Sun. by chance.
4 miles east of Alanson.

25 Second Hand Man & The Flea Marketers
7493 U.S. 31
Alanson , MI 49706
616 548-5173
Summer: Every Day 11 to 5; Winter: By chance.
East side of highway.

ODEN

26 DC - DOE Antiques
4577 U.S. 31 North (Moving in 1995 - call for location.)
Oden , MI 49764
616 347-0234
Memorial Day to Labor Day: Every Day 11 to 5;
Oct. & May: Sat. & Sun. 11 to 5, weekdays by chance.
North side of road 2 doors south of park. Art deco.

BRUTUS

27 Adams Antiques
U.S. 31
Brutus , MI 49716
616 529-6596
May to mid-Oct.: Mon. to Sat. 11 to 5;
Mid-Oct. to April by chance or appointment.
East side of highway, just north of Brutus.

28 Graham's Antiques
1812 Gregory Road
Brutus, MI 49716
616 539-8275
Mid-May to Mid-Oct.: Every day 9 a.m. to 9 p.m.
From U.S. 31 between Brutus and Pellston go east 1 mile on Woodland to Gregory, go right a quarter mile to shop.

PELLSTON

29 Town & Country Antiques
U.S. 31
Pellston , MI 49769
616 539-8430; (res.: 616 539-8542)
June to Sept. 15: Every day 10 to 5
Downtown, east side os street.

LEVERING

30 Gaslight Antiques & Collectibles
7116 N. U.S. 31
Levering, MI 49755
616 537-4446
Mid-May thru Oct.: Daily 10 to 5:30
East side of highway, 2 miles north of Levering blinker light.
Wicker, pottery, dishes, and general line of antiques.

31 Levering Antiques & Rustic Furniture
Robinson Street
Levering , MI 49755
616 537-4972
May to Sept.; by appointment in winter.
Downtown, 3 blocks west of U.S. 31, near from post office

32 Little Bit Country
7010 U.S. 31
Levering , MI 49755
616 537-2525
May 1 through Oct.: Daily 9 to 5:30;
Nov. & Dec.: weekends or by chance.
Between Levering and Carp Lake.
Antiques, collectibles, hand-made crafts and country items.

CARP LAKE

33 Old Tyme Treasures
6478 Gill Road
Carp Lake , MI 49718
616 537-2229
Mid-May to Mid-Oct. Daily 10 to 5; Sun. 12 to 5
On U.S. 31 at light.
6 dealer co-op.

34 The Maples Resort & Antiques
8982 Paradise Trail (Old U.S. 31)
Carp Lake , MI 49718
616 537-4814
April to Nov.: Every day & evenings.
Between Mackinaw City and Carp Lake, 5 miles south of Mackinaw City.
Glassware, bronze, & general line.

10.5 CHEBOYGAN COUNTY

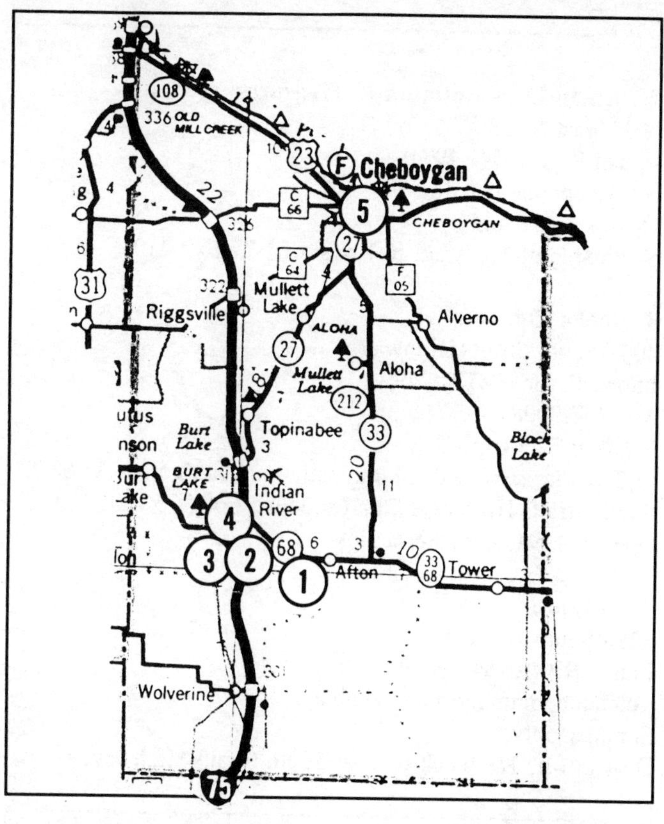

For Additional Information:
* Cheboygan Chamber of Commerce, 616 627-5841

AFTON

1 Hill Top Antiques
638 Onaway (M-68)
Afton MI 49705
Every day 10:30 to 4:30
South side of highway, 6 miles east of Indian River.

INDIAN RIVER

2 Bearly Used Antiques & Treasures
6033 East M-68
Indian River, MI 49749
No Telephone listed.
Open summer only.
South side of highway, just west of I-75 Exit 310.

3 Books Etc.
4041 South Straits Highway
Indian River, MI 49749
616 238-9008
Mon. to Sat. 10 to 6
In The Plaza, little shopping mall, southeast corner M-68 & South Straits Highway, a half mile west of I-75 Exit 310.
Opened 1994; books & antiques.

4 Antiques
6288 South Avenue
Indian River, MI 49749
Telephone number not available.
Summer only.
Downtown, 1/2 block west of South Straits Highway.

CHEBOYGAN

5 Antiques & Collectibles
211 N. Main Street
Cheboygan, MI 49721
616 627-7237
Mon. to Sat. 10 to 5
Downtown, across from the post office.
Lamp parts & restoration.

TIER 11
THE UPPER PENINSULA

11.01 MACKINAC COUNTY

MAP: MACKINAC COUNTY & CHIPPEWA COUNTY

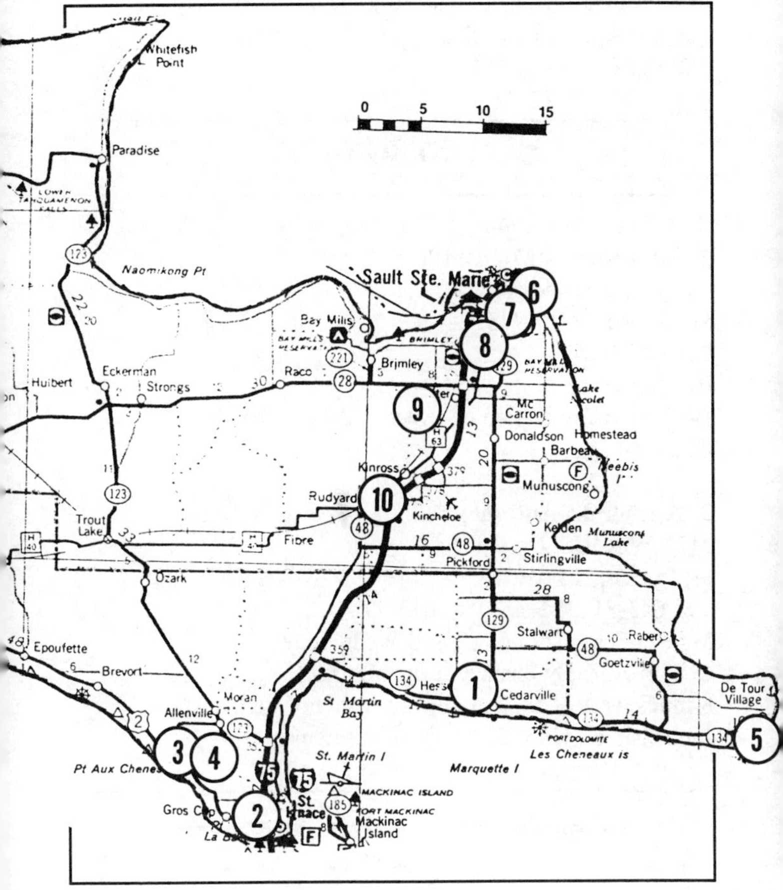

Recommended Points of Interest:

* Tahquamenon Falls State Park, Paradise

* S.S. Valley Camp and Maritime Museum, Sault Ste. Marie, 906-632-3658

For Additional Information:

* St. Ignace Chamber of Commerce, 906 643-8717

* Sault Area Chamber of Commerce, 906 643-8717

CEDARVILLE

1 The Woodshed Gift Shop
M-134 & M-129
Cedarville, MI 49719
906 484-3002
May to Dec.: Mon. to Sat. 10 to 5;
Jan. to Apr.: Fri. & Sat. 10 to 5
1/2 block south of light.

ST IGNACE

2 Miss Ellen's Mercantile
404 North State Street
St. Ignace, MI 49781
906 643-9274
By chance.
Downtown, west side of street, 1/2 block south of Goudreau.

3 Anchor In Antiques
2122 West US 2
St. Ignace, MI 49781
906 643-8112; Res.: 906 643-9917
May to Sep: 10 to 5, Closed Wednesday
Oct. to Apr: By chance or appointment.
8 miles west of St. Ignace, north side of highway.
Emphasis on Great Lakes Nautical Items.

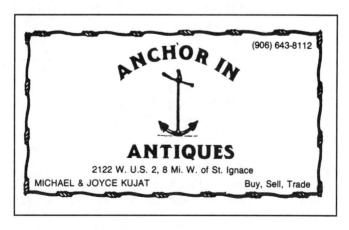

4 Superior Paper Company
2122 West U.S. 2 - Unit 1
St. Ignace, MI 49781
906 643-8122
Memorial Day to Labor Day: Thurs. to Tues. 10 to 5
In back of Anchor In Antiques; U.S. 2 west of St. Ignace.
Military & paper collectibles.

11.02 CHIPPEWA COUNTY

(Map in Preceding Section)

DE TOUR VILLAGE

5 Log Cabin Antiques & Collectibles
637 Ontario Street
De Tour Village, MI 49725
906 297-2502
May to Oct.: Mon. to Sat. 9 to 5
Across from the marina.
No crafts or reproductions.

SAULT STE. MARIE

6 Gran & Gramps Antiques & Collectibles
506 East Portage Avenue
Sault Ste. Marie, MI 49783
906 632-4256
June 1 to Sept. 30: Mon. to Sat. 12 to 6
Winter: Sat. 12 to 6
From the north end of downtown go east on Portage Street
5 blocks; south side of street.

7 Hoffman's Antique Shoppe
514 Emeline Street
Sault Ste. Marie, MI 49783
906 632-0906; res.: 906 632-8769
April to Dec.: Mon. to Sat. 10 to 6;
Jan. to March: Thurs. to Sat. 11 to 5
(Recently moved from Portage Ave.)

8 La Galerie
1420 Ashmun Street
Sault Ste. Marie, MI 49783
906 635-1044
Mon. to Sat. 10 to 5
Southwest corner Sixth Ave. & Ashmun, south of downtown, on I-75 Business Spur.

BRIMLEY

9 Willow Grove Farms
M-28, Rt. 2 Box 45
Brimley, MI 49715
906 248-5168
April to Dec. 31: Thurs. to Sun. 11 to 5
4 miles west of I-75, south side of highway, down a long dirt road.
Antiques, herbs, flowers.

RUDYARD

10 Northern Heritage Antiques & Collectibles
Tilson Road, Rte. 1, Box 789
Rudyard, MI 49780
906 478-3507
May 14 to Oct. 15: Tues. to Sat. 10 to 5
From I-75 west to stop sign, then north one mile.

11.03 LUCE COUNTY

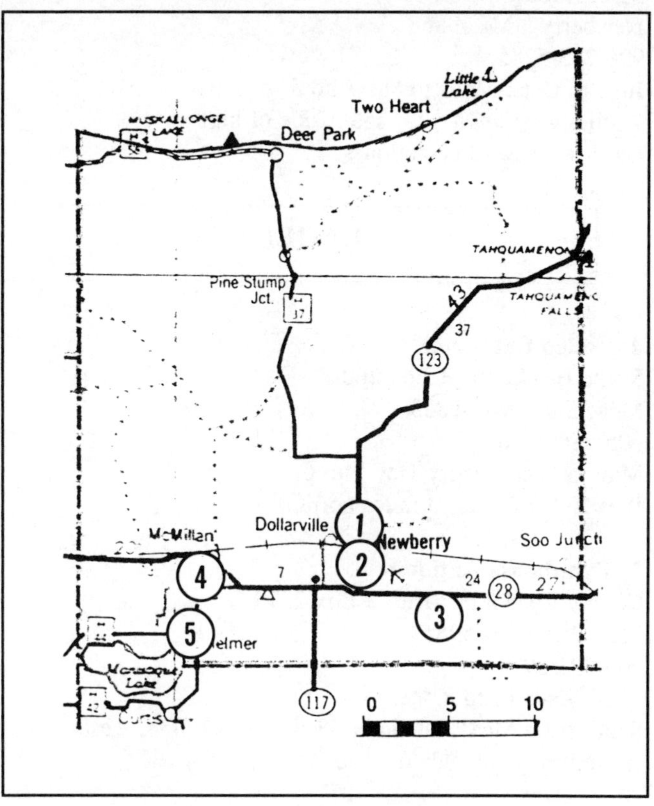

NEWBERRY

1 Antiques By Donelle
101 East John Street
Newberry, MI 49868
906 293-8044; res.: 906 586-9544
Tues. to Fri. 10 to 5, or by appointment; closed March.

2 Country Gallery
607 Newberry Avenue (MI Route 123)
Newberry , MI 49868
906 293-8262
June to Oct.: Mon to Sat. 9 a.m. to 10 p.m.;
Winter: Mon. to Fri. 8 to 6, Sat. 9:30 to 6
South of downtown, east side of street.
Mostly gifts, some antiques.

3 Sage River Trading Post
M-28, Route 1 Box 644
Newberry, MI 49868
906 293-5285
June to Oct.: Mon. to Sat. 9 to 5
7 miles west of M-123, south side of highway.
Used items & some antiques.

McMILLAN

4 Calico Cat
Route H-33, Rt. 3 Box 2609
McMillan, MI 49853
906 586-3918
May to Sept.: Every Day 9 to 6
West side of road, 3 miles north of Curtis.

5 Farmhouse Antiques
County Road 438, Rte. 3 Box 2279
McMillan, MI 49853
906 293-8972
Every day: 10 to 8
South from McMillan on H-33 to Co. Rd. 438, west on 438 two miles; south side of road.

11.04 SCHOOLCRAFT COUNTY

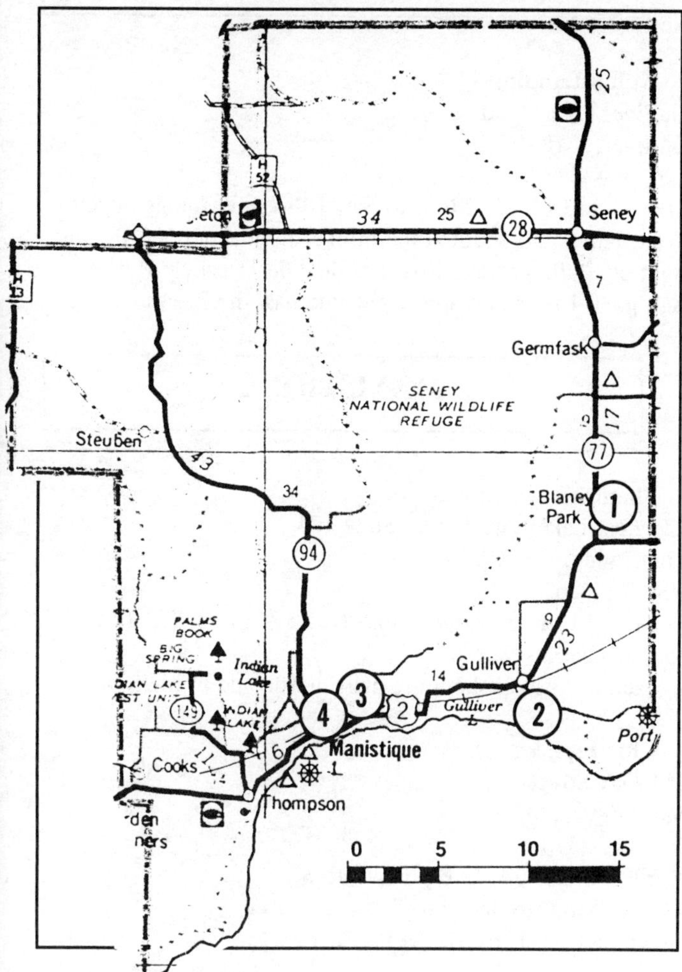

For Additional Information:
* Schoolcraft County Chamber of Commerce, 906 341-5010

BLANEY PARK

1 Paul Bunyan's Country Store
RR 1, Box 57
Blaney Park , MI 49836
906 283-3861
May 1 to Dec.1: Mon. to Sat. 8:30 to 8; Sun. 10 to 8
1 mile north of U.S. 2 on M-77.

GULLIVER

2 Gull's Landing
Gulliver Lake Road
Gulliver, MI 49840
906 283-3373
May 15 to Oct. 15: Mon. to Sat. 10 to 5; evenings by apt.
From U.S. 2 go south at the blinker light about 500 ft., turn right on Gulliver Lake Road; at the Old Deerfield Resort sign go 1/4 mile down on right side past the Resort.

MANISTIQUE

3 Phanlasmagoria
726 East Lakeshore Drive, Suite 104
Manistique, MI 49854
906 341-6262
Memorial Day weekend to mid-Nov.: Mon. to Fri. 12 to 7, Sat. by chance 12 to 6
In back of a small shopping mall, north side of highway.

4 Christophers
211 Oak Street
Manistique, MI
906 341-2570
April 1 to Dec 24: Every day 9 to 8;
Winter: Mon. to Sat. 9 to 5
Downtown, just east of the post office.

11.05 ALGIER COUNTY

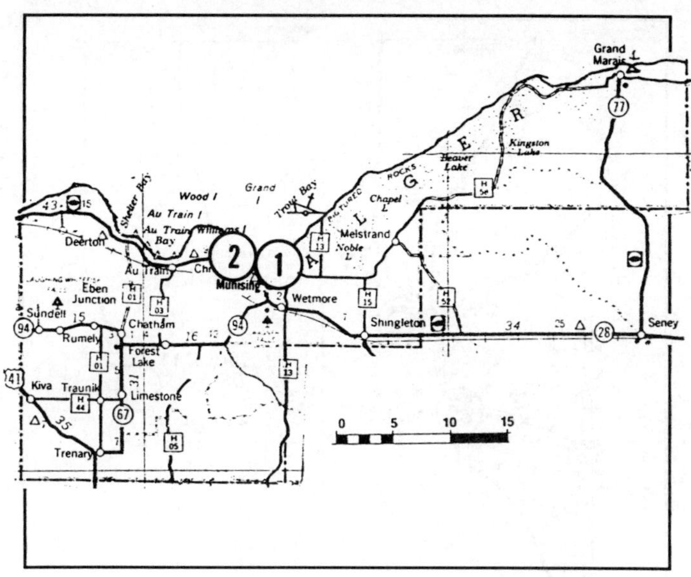

Recommended Points of Interest:
* Pictured Rocks National Lakeshore, Munising
* Alger County Historical Museum, Munising, 906-4186

For Additional Information:
* Alger Chamber of Commerce, 906 387-2138

MUNISING

1 The Bay House
111 Elm Avenue
Munising, MI 49862
906 387-4253
Summer: Mon. to Sat. 10 to 7; Sun. 12 to 5
Winter: Tues. to Sat. 10 to 5
Go south at First Peoples Bank.

2 Old North Light Antiques & Gifts
M-28 West
Munising, MI 49862
906 387-2109
Open 7 days 9 to 9
Gifts in front, antiques in back.

11.06 DELTA COUNTY

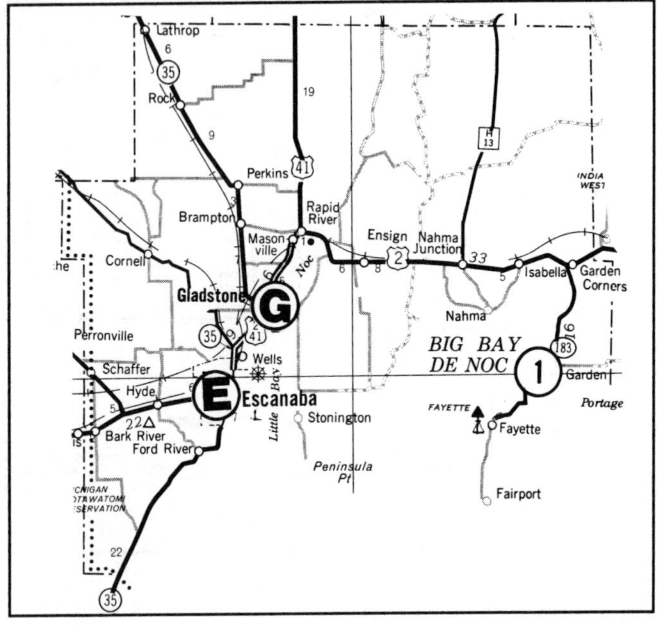

G. Gladstone: 2 to 5
E. Escanaba: 6 to 10

Recommended Points of Interest:
* Fayette Historic State Park, Garden, 906 644-2603 (19th Century iron smelting company town)
* Garden Peninsula Historical Museum, Garden, 906 644-2695
* William Bonifas Fine Arts Center, 700 First Avenue South, 906 493-5500

For Additional Information:
* Delta County Chamber of Commerce, 906 786-2192

GARDEN

1 Antiques in the Garden
MI Route 183
Garden, MI 49835
906 644-2727; 906 644-2348
Memorial Day to Sept. 30: Every day 12 to 5
Downtown

GLADSTONE

2 Reflections (Restaurant with antiques for sale.)
1016 Delta Avenue
Gladstone, MI 49837
906 428-1134
Tues. to Fri. 10 to 7, Sat. & Sun. 10 to 4
West end of downtown, north side of street.

3 Chicken Coop Antiques
7051 P Road
Gladstone, MI 49837
906 786-1150
May to Nov.: Every Day 12 to 5
From U.S. 41 south of town go east on P Road four blocks; west side of road, just north of 183rd Road. Small shed.

4 Fort Wells Antiques
(Bay View Furniture Stripping & Antiques)
7097 P Road
Gladstone, MI 49837
906 786-4264
Open year round.
From U.S. 41 south of town go east on P Road two blocks; west side of road across and a block south of The Terrace.

5 Foxx Den Antiques
7509 U.S. 2 & 41 & M35
Gladstone , MI 49837
906 786-9014
Tues. to Fri. 10 to 5, other days by chance.
Small building back of garage, west side of highway.

ESCANABA

6 Queen's Ransom (formerly Peddlers Alley)
223 Ludington
Escanaba, MI 49826
906 786-8581
Summer: Tues. to Sat. 10 to 6, Sun. 11 to 3;
Winter: Tues. to Sat. 11 to 5, Sun. 11 to 3
Downtown

11.06 Delta County - continued

7 The Market Place
500 Ludington Street
Escanaba, MI 49829
906 789-1326
Mon. to Sat. 10 to 5; Easter to Christmas also open Sun. 12 to 4
Downtown
Co-op shop; opened 1985; 25 dealers.

8 The Belle Pearl
519 Ludington Street
Escanaba, MI 49829
906 789-0041; 906 786-4919
Mon. to Fri. 11:30 to 5:30; Sat. 11:30 to 3
Downtown, south side of street.

9 Past and Presents
1200 Ludington Street
Escanaba, MI 49829
906 786-1757
Mon. to Sat. 10 to 5
Antiques and hand crafted gifts.

10 U.P. Treasure Hunters Antique Mall
1812 Ludington
Escanaba, MI 49829
No telephone listed.
Open year round, Daily 10 to 6
5 Blocks East of US 2 & 41 Intersection, north side of street.
12,000 square feet; one of the few malls in the U.P.

11.07 MENOMINEE COUNTY

MAP: MENOMINEE & DICKINSON COUNTIES

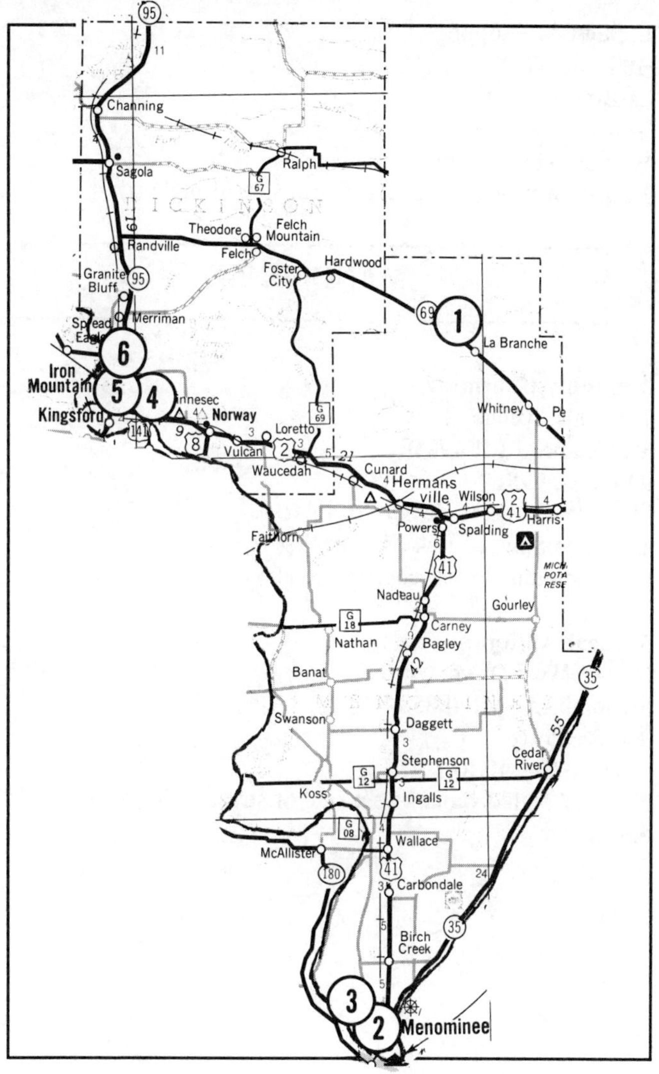

Recommended Points of Interest:

* IXL Museum, Hermansville, 906-498-2410

* Cornish Pump & Mining Museum, Iron Mountain, 906 774-1086

For Additional Information:

* Menominee Chamber of Commerce, 906 863-2679

* Dickinson County Chamber of Comm. 906 774-2002

LA BRANCHE

1 Sheba's Shoppe
Highway 69 West
La Branche, MI
906 246-3596
Mon. & Tues. or by appointment.
2 miles west of La Branche, north side of highway.

MENOMINEE

2 Simply Charming
111 10th Avenue
Menominee, MI 49858
906 863-5995
Mon. to Fri. 12 to 5, Sat. 10 to 4;
also open Sun. 12 to 4 May to Sept.
Crafts, florals, brass, copper, jewelry.

3 Ideal Antiques
N. 145 West Drive
Menominee, MI 49858
906 863-5918
Mon. to Sat. 10 to 5
North of 18th Avenue, west side of street. Northwest of downtown.

11.08 DICKINSON COUNTY

(Map in Preceding Section)

IRON MOUNTAIN

4 House of Yesteryear Museum
W-7764 U.S. 2
Iron Mountain, MI 49801
906 774-0789
June to Sept.: Tues., Thurs., Sat. 10 to 5
East side of town, north side of highway.

5 Carriage Oak Antiques & Gifts
103 West "A" Street
Iron Mountain, MI 49801
906 774-5777
Mon. to Fri. 10 to 5; Sat. 10 to 3:30
Downtown, 1 block west of U.S. 2, south side of street.
Antiques and gifts.

6 Cobweb Antiques
N-3956 North US-2
Iron Mountain, MI 49801
906 774-6560
Mon. to Sat. 1 to 4, or by appointment.
Just south of the M-95 & U.S. 2 junction, northeast side of street.

11.09 MARQUETTE COUNTY

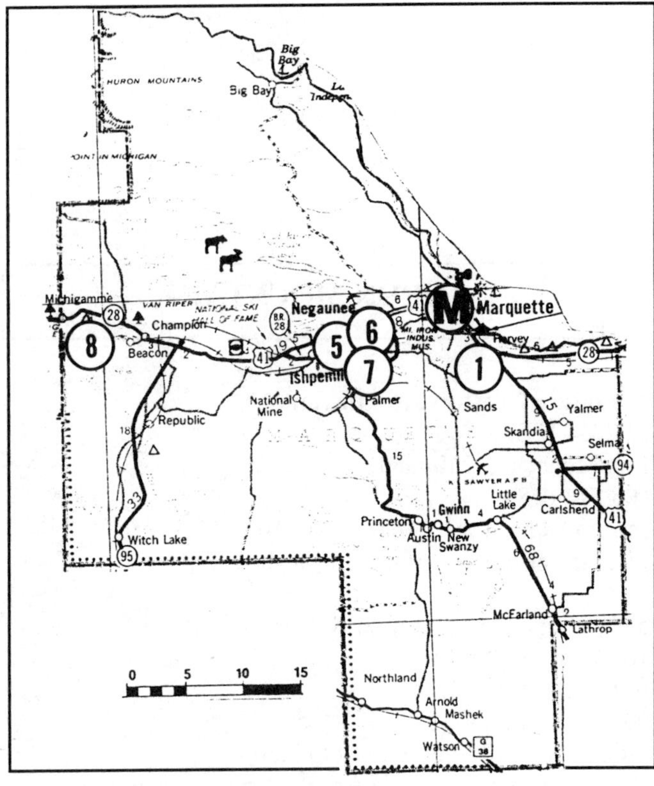

M: 2 to 4 - Marquette, see Detail Map

Recommended Points of Interest:
* Negaunee Michigan Iron Industry Museum, 906 475-7857
* Maritime Museum, Marquette, 906 226-2006
* Vierling 1883 Saloon, 119 S. Front, Marquette

For Additional Information:
* Marquette County Chamber of Commerce, 906 228-7749

HARVEY

1 Antique Village
2296 U.S. 41 South
Harvey , MI 49855
906 249-3040
May 1 to Dec. 24: Mon. to Sat. 10 to 6, Sun. 12 to 5
West side of highway, north of M-28 & U.S. 41 junction.

MARQUETTE

2 The Collector Antiques
214 South Front
Marquette, MI 49855
906 228-4134
Mon. to Sat. 10 to 5:30, Sun. 12 to 4
Downtown, west side of street.

3 Fagan's Antiques
219 West Washington
Marquette, MI 49855
906 228-4311
Mon. to Sat. 11 to 5, Sun. 12 to 4
Downtown, south side of street.
(May be moving in 1995.)

DETAIL MAP: MARQUETTE

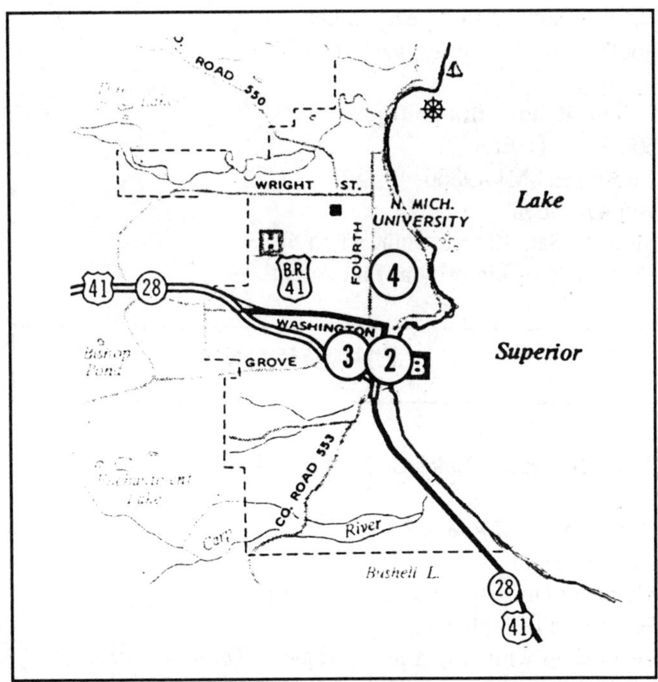

4 The Yankee Peddler
611 North Third Street
Marquette, MI 49855
906 226-2973
Mon. to Fri. 11 to 5, Sat. 11 to 3
North of downtown, east side of street.

NEGAUNEE

5 Old Bank Building Antiques
331 Iron
Negaunee, MI 49866
906 475-4777
Mon. to Sat. 10 to 5, Sun. 12 to 4
Downtown

6 Kate's Collectibles
28 U.S. 41 East
Negaunee, MI 49866
906 475-4443
Open 7 days 12 to 5 year 'round
South side of highway, east of town.

7 The Renovators Antiques
600 U.S. 41 East
Negaunee, MI 49866
906 475-5600
Mon. to Sat. 10 to 6, Sun. 11 to 5
North side of highway at Pine Street.

CHAMPION

8 Michigamme Lake Lodge Gift Shop
U.S. 41
Champion, MI 49814
906 339-4400
May 1 to Oct. 30: Whenever lodge is open.
South side of highway.
Small shop with only a few antiques. The rustic 1934 lodge, however, is worth staying at if at all possible.

11.10 IRON COUNTY

MAP: IRON & BARAGA COUNTIES

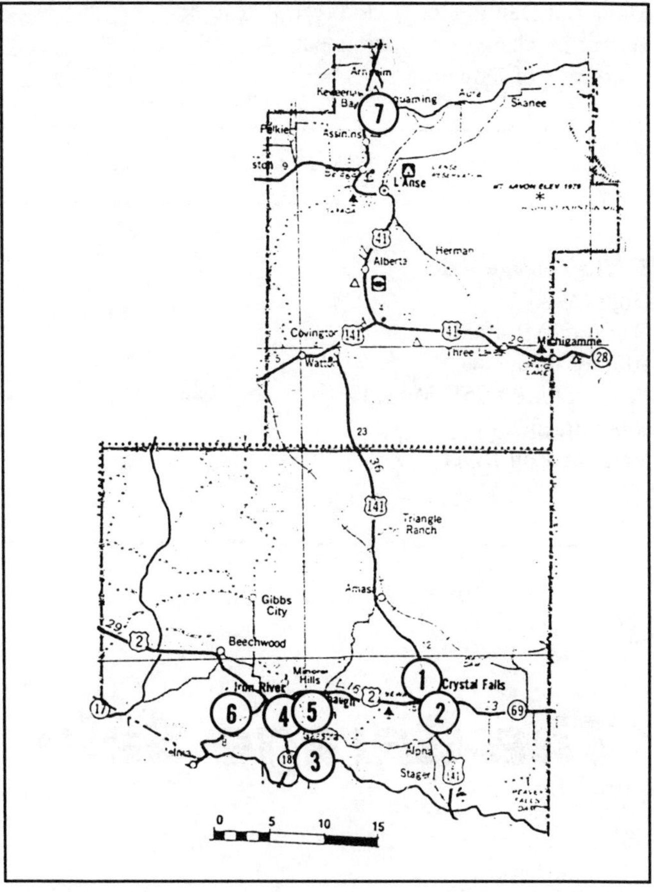

For Additional Information:
* Iron County Chamber of Commerce, 906 254-3822

CRYSTAL FALLS

1 Bargain Barn Antiques
1340 West US-2
Crystal Falls, MI 49920
906 875-3381
Thurs. to Mon. 10 to 5
North side of highway, west end of town.

2 Old Tradition Shop
612 Michigan Avenue
Crystal Falls, MI 49920
906 875-4214
Memorial Day to Oct. 1: Every Day 9 to 5;
Winter by chance or appointment.
Southwest of Downtown.

GAASTRA

3 The Garage Sale
Highway 424
Gaastra, MI 49927
906 265-9765
Fri. to Sun.8 to 5; Mon. to Thurs. by chance or appointment.
South of Iron River.

IRON RIVER

4 Ethel Joyce Turbessi at the Antique Cottage
545 West Ice Lake Road
Iron River, MI 49935
906 265-9753 or 906 265-2756
Open by chance.
South from U.S. 2 at red & yellow Lakeshore Motel sign.

5 Apple Orchard Antiques
1603 Kofmehl Road
Iron River, MI 49935
906 265-9723
June 1 to Oct. 1: By chance
From U.S. 2 East go south on Bates Gaastra Road, just east of a school. Continue two miles; road becomes Kofmehl Road. East side of road.

6 Sophie's Antiques
101 Meadow View Drive
Iron River, MI 49935
906 265-5978
Sun. 12:30 to 7
2 miles west of town, 2 miles south of U.S. 2.

11.11 BARAGA COUNTY

(Map in preceding section.)

Recommended Points of Interest:
* Hanka 1896 Finnish Homestead, Baraga, 906 353-7116

For Additional Information:
* Baraga Tourist Association, 906 534-7116

BARAGA

7 The Country Shop
Rte. 1 Box 66
Baraga, MI
906 353-7230
By chance.
5 miles north of Baraga on Jurmu Road off U.S. 41.
Small house in back of garage.

11.12 GOGEBIC COUNTY

MAP: GOGEBIC & ONTONAGON COUNTIES

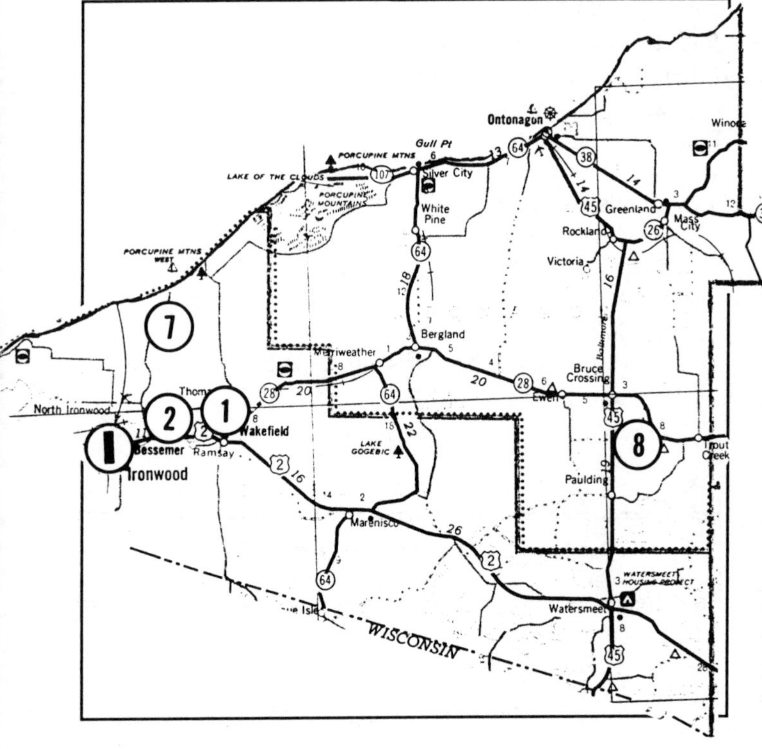

I: 3 to 6 - Ironwood

Recommended Points of Interest:
* Porcupine Mountains Wilderness Park, Ontonagon

For Additional Information:
* Gogebic Visitors Bureau, 906 885-5275
* Ontonagon County Chamber of Commerce, 906 885-5275

RAMSAY

1 U.S. 2 Antiques
U.S. 2 & Blackjack Road
Ramsay, MI
906 667-0642; 906 667-0681
Tues. to Fri. 10 to 5; also Sun. June to Aug.
2 miles east of Bessemer, north side of U.S. 2.

BESSEMER

2 Sellar Street Antiques
114 East Sellar Street
Bessemer, MI 49911
906 667-0191
Mon. Thurs. & Sat. 11 to 4
Downtown, 3 blocks south of U.S. 2

IRONWOOD

3 The Depot Antiques
316 Lake Street
Ironwood, MI 49938
906 932-0900
Summer: Mon. to Sat. 9 to 5, Sun. 11 to 4;
Winter: Mon. to Sat. 10 to 4
East side Ironwood a block south of US 2, east side of street.

4 Doreen's Antiques
313 Lake Street
Ironwood, MI 49938
906 932-4310
Mon. to Sat. 10 to 4

5 The Village Store
701 East McLeod Avenue
Ironwood , MI 49938
906 932-5394
Summer: Mon. to Sat. 10:30 to 4;
Winter: 11 to 4
From U.S. 2 east of Ironwood go south on Lake Street, which becomes McLeod Avenue; south side of street.

6 The Carriage House Antiques
303 South Lowell
Ironwood, MI 49938
906 932-0766; 906 932-2710 res.
Downtown

7 The Net Loft Antiques
Black River Road
Ironwood, MI 49938
906 932-3660
From U.S. 2 east of Ironwood north on Powderhorn Road, past Airport Road to Black River Road, north ten miles.

11.13 ONTONAGON COUNTY

(Map in preceding section.)

BRUCE CROSSING

8 Northern Lights Antiques & Artisans
575 Himanka Hill Road
Bruce Crossing, MI 49912
906 827-3933
May 15 to Sept. 15: Every Day 11 to 5;
Winter by chance.
South on U.S. 45 4 miles from Mich. Route 28, then east .9 mile. North side of road in brown metal building.

11.14 HOUGHTON COUNTY

MAP: HOUGHTON & KEWEENAW COUNTIES

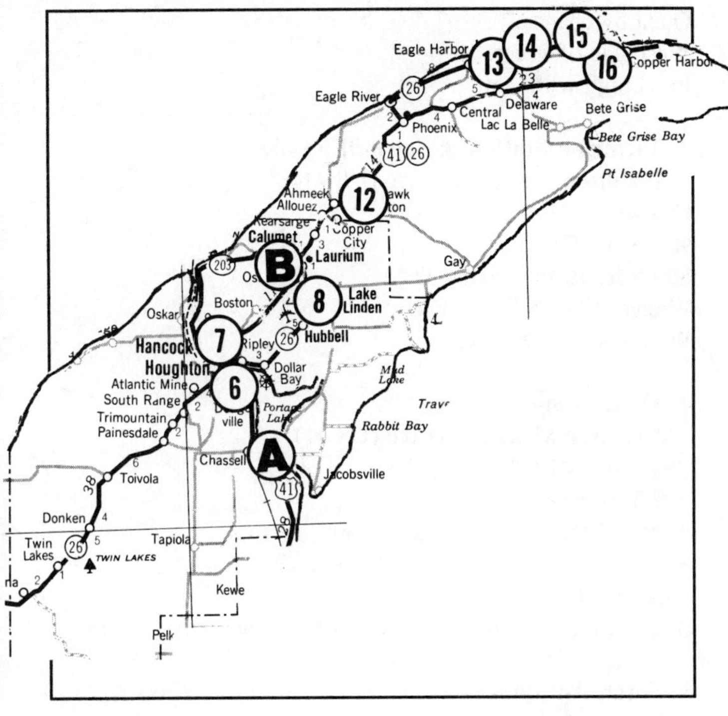

A: Chassel - 1 to 5
B: Calumet - 9 to 11

Recommended Points of Interest:
* Shute's 1890 bar, 322 6th Street, Calumet

For Additional Information:
* Keweenaw Tourism Council, 906 482-2388

CHASSELL

1 Eagle Shop
148 N. Wilson Drive (U.S. 41)
Chassell, MI 49916
906 523-4423
May 1 to Oct. 30: Mon. to Sat. 9:30 to 5:30
North end of town, west side of highway.

2 Grandma's Antiques
300 Wilson Memorial Drive (U.S. 41)
Chassell, MI 49916
No telephone listed.
Open by chance.
West side of street.
Piled high with stuff.

3 Victorian Station & Sawmill Resale
414 Willson Memorial Drive (US 41)
Chassell, MI 49916
906 523-4729
Summer: 10 to 8 Every Day;
Winter: 10 to 5 Every Day
West side of the street.

4 Einerlei Shop
422 Willson Memorial Drive (US 41)
Chassell, MI 49916
906 523-4612
Winter: Mon. to Sat. 10 to 5, Sun. 11 to 5
Summer: Mon. to Sat. 9 to 6, Sun. 10 to 5
West side of the street.
Gifts, home furnishings, herb garden, some vintage items.

5 Porch Antiques
447 U.S. 41
Chassell, MI 49916
906 523-4819
Mar. 1 to Dec.1: Mon. to Sat. 10 to 5
West side of highway, north side of town.

HOUGHTON

6 Antique Mall
418 Sheldon Avenue
Houghton, MI 49931
906 487-9483
June 1 to Sept. 1: Mon. to Fri. 10 to 6, Sat. 10 to 5;
Winter: Mon. to Sat. 10 to 5
Downtown

HANCOCK

7 Northwoods Trading Post
120 Quincy
Hancock, MI 49930
906 482-5210
Mon. to Thurs. 9:30 to 5:30; Fri. 9:30 to 6; Sat. 9:30 to 5
Downtown south side of street.

LAKE LINDEN

8 Treasured Friends Antiques
313 Calumet Street
Lake Linden, MI 49945
906 296-0184; res.: 906 296-0604
July & Aug.: Mon. to Sat. 12:30 to 4:30

CALUMET

9 Copper World
101 Fifth Street
Calumet, MI 49913
906 337-4016
July 4 to Labor Day: Mon. to Sat. 9 to 8;
Winter: Mon. to Sat. 9:30 to 5
Downtown New and old copper items.

10 Del's Antiques
308 Fifth Street Downtown
Calumet, MI 49913
906 337-3972 May to Oct.: Mon. to Sat. 12 to 5

11 The Rose & The Thorn
451 Pine
Calumet, MI 49913
906 337-1717
May to Oct.: Mon. to Fri. 9 to 9, Sat. 9 to 5, Sun. 12 to 5;
Winter: Mon. to Sat. 10 to 5, Sun. by chance
North end of downtown; NEC 5th & Pine Streets.
Ceramics & gifts 1st floor, antiques in basement.

11.15 KEWEENAW COUNTY

(Map in preceding section.)

Recommended Points of Interest:
* Fort Wilkins Historic Complex, Copper Harbor
* Keweenaw Mountain Lodge, Copper Harbor

For Additional Information:
* Keweenaw Tourism Council, 906 482-2388

ALLOUEZ

12 The Last Place on Earth
U.S. 41
Allouez, MI 49805
906 337-1014
May 1 to Oct. 15: Every Day 9 to 5
West side of highway, 3 miles north of Calumet.

EAGLE HARBOR

13 The Museum Shop
Route 1 Box 190
Eagle Harbor, MI 49950
906 289-4911
May 27th to Sept. 30th: Mon. to Sat. 10 to 6, Sun. 2 to 5
North side of highway, east side of town, on the grounds of the Eagle Harbor Light House.
Specializing in copper items and Victorian transferware.

14 Chit Chat Antiques & Collectibles
24 Sand Dunes Road
Eagle Harbor, MI 49950
906 289-4913
Mon. to Sat. 10 to 5, Sun. 12 to 5
Just north on MI Route 26.

COPPER HARBOR

15 Log Cabin Gifts
MI Route 26
Copper Harbor, MI 49918
906 289-4560
June 1 to Sept. 1: Every Day 10 to 6
South side of road, 4 miles west of Copper Harbor.

16 Minnetonka's Aster House Museum
U.S. 41 & MI Route 26
Copper Harbor, MI
906 289-4449
May 15 to Oct. 15: Every day 9 to 6
Center of town.
Antique shop & museum in back of the motel.

SELECTED ANTIQUE SHOWS IN WESTERN MICHIGAN

SEPTEMBER 1994

Sat. to Mon. September 3 to 5: Cornwell's Turkeyville Flea Market, 18935 15 1/2 Mile Rd., Marshall. Hours: 11 to 8. 616 781-4293

Monday September 5 (Labor Day): Burley Park Antique & Collectible Market, Howard City. Mon. 8 to 4. Admission: $1.50. 616 354-6354

Sat. & Sun. September 10 & 11: Marshall Home Tour; antique market at B.E. Henry Building, Calhoun County Fairgrounds, and Marshall Middle School. Sat. 9 to 5, Sun. 10 to 5. 616 781-5163

Sat. & Sun. September 10 & 11: Dolls, Dolls, Dolls Show, Cook Energy Information Center, I-94 exit 16, 3 1/2 miles north on Red Arrow Highway, Bridgeman. Admission: FREE. 800 548-2555

Sat. & Sun. September 10 & 11: Spring Antique Festival, Williamston. Sat. 9 to 6, Sun. 10 to 4. 517 655-2622

Sat. & Sun. September 17 & 18: Marshall Antique Market, Calhoun County Fairgrounds, intersection of I-94 & I69, Marshall. Sat. 8 to 4, Sun. 10 to 4. Admission: $3.00. 616 789-0990

Sunday September 18: Ionia Antique & Collectible Market, Ionia Fairgrounds, South M-66, Ionia. Sun. 8 to 4:30. Admission: $2.00. 517 593-3316

Sat. to Sun. September 24 & 25: Cornwell's Turkeyville Flea Market, 18935 15 1/2 Mile Rd., Marshall. Hours: 11 to 8. 616 781-4293

Sunday September 25: Allegan Antique Market, Allegan Fairgrounds, Allegan. Sun. 7:30 to 4:30. 616 453-8780

Thur. to Sun. September 29 to October 2: Meridian Mall, 1982 E. Grand River Avenue, Okemos. During regular mall hours. 616 629-3133

OCTOBER 1994

Sat. & Sun. October 1 & 2: Stamp & Coin Collectors Show, Cook Energy Information Center, I-94 exit 16, 3 1/2 miles north on Red Arrow Highway, Bridgeman. Admission: FREE. 800 548-2555

October 1994, continued:
Sunday October 2: Burley Park Antique & Collectible Market, Howard City. Mon. 8 to 4. Admission: $1.50. 616 354-6354

Sat. & Sun. October 8 & 9: Heritage Hill Antiques Festival, Ford Fieldhouse, Grand Rapids. 616 629-3133

Sunday October 9: Caravan Antiques Market, Fairgrounds on Rt 86, Centerville. Sun. 7 to 4. Admission: $3.00. 312 227-4464

Sat. & Sun. October 15 & 16: Antique Show, Cook Energy Information Center, I-94 exit 16, 3 1/2 miles north on Red Arrow Highway, Bridgeman. Admission: FREE. 800 548-2555

Sat. & Sun. October 15 & 16: Marshall Antique Market, Calhoun County Fairgrounds, intersection of I-94 & I69, Marshall. Sat. 8 to 4, Sun. 10 to 4. Admission: $3.00. 616 789-0990

Sat. & Sun. October 15 & 16: Superfest Collector's Event, Ingham County Fairgrounds, Mason. Sat. 8 to 6, Sun. 9 to 4. Admission: $3.00. 517 676-2079

Sat. & Sun. October 22 & 23: Collectors' Showcase, Stadium Arena, 2500 Turner St., Grand Rapids. Sat. 10 to 7, Sun. 10 to 5. 616 629-3133

Sat. & Sun., Oct. 22 & 23: Fall Festival Antique Show & Sale, West Shore Community College, 3000 North Shore Road, Scottsville. Sat. 10 to 8, Sun. 11 to 5. $2.00 admission. 616 845-0450 or 616 845-7414.

Sunday October 23: Ionia Antique & Collectible Market, Ionia Fairgrounds, South M-66, Ionia. Sun. 8 to 4:30. Admission: $2.00. 517 593-3316

Sat. & Sun. October 29 & 30: The Barry Expo Center Antique Show, M-37 south from 28th St. SE and Woodland Mall, Middleville. Sat. 10 to 9, Sun. 10 to 6. Admission: $2.00. 616 453-8780.

NOVEMBER 1994

Sat. & Sun. November 26 & 27: Holiday Collectors' Showcase, Lansing Center, Lansing. 616 629-3133

JANUARY 1995

Thur. to Sun. January 26 to 29: Meridian Mall, Lansing. 616 629-3133

FEBRUARY 1995

Sat. & Sun. February 11 & 12: Winter FunFest Antique Show, Ramada Inn & Convention Center, 4079 West U.S. 10, Ludington.

Sat. & Sun. February 11 & 12: Collectors' Showcase, Stadium Arena, 2500 Turner St., Grand Rapids. Sat. 10 to 7, Sun. 10 to 5. 616 629-3133

MARCH 1995

Sunday March 5: Grand Rapids Antique Bottle & Glass Show, Grand Rapids. Sun. 9 to 3. Admission: $1.00 Donation. 616 457-6448

Sat. & Sun. March 11 & 12: The Barry Expo Center Antique Show, M-37 south from 28th St. SE and Woodland Mall, Middleville. Sat. 10 to 9, Sun. 10 to 6. Admission: $2.00. 616 453-8780.

APRIL 1995

Sat. & Sun. April 15 & 16: Marshall Antiques Market, Calhoun County Fairgrounds, Marshall. Sat. 8 to 4, Sun. 10 to 4. Admission: $3.00. 616 789-0990

Sat. & Sun. April 29 & 30: Spring Antique Show, Cook Energy Information Center, I-94 exit 16, 3 1/2 miles north on Red Arrow Highway, Bridgeman. Admission: FREE. 800 548-2555

Sunday April 30: Allegan Antique Market, Allegan Fairgrounds, Allegan. Sun. 7:30 to 4:30. 616 453-8780

MAY 1995

Sat. & Sun. May 6 & 7: Spring Antique Festival, Downtown Williamston. 517 676-9227

Sunday May 7: Caravan Antiques Market, Fairgrounds on Rt 86, Centerville. Sun. 7 to 4. Admission: $3.00. 312 227-4464

Sat. & Sun. May 13 & 14: Marshall Antiques Market, Calhoun County Fairgrounds, Marshall. Sat. 8 to 4, Sun. 10 to 4. Admission: $3.00. 616 789-0990

Sat. & Sun. May 20 & 21: Superfest Collectors Event, Ingham County Fairgrounds, Mason. Sat. 8 to 6, Sun. 9 to 4. Admission: $3.00. 517 676-2079

May 1995, continued:
Sunday May 28: Allegan Antique Market, Allegan Fairgrounds, Allegan. Sun. 7:30 to 4:30. 616 453-8780

Monday May 29 (Memorial Day): Burley Park Antique & Collectible Market, Howard City. Mon. 8 to 4. Admission: $1.50. 616 354-6354

JUNE 1995

Thurs. to Sun. June 1 to 4: Meridian Mall, Lansing. 616 629-3133

Sunday June 11: Caravan Antiques Market, Fairgrounds on Rt 86, Centerville. Sun. 7 to 4. Admission: $3.00. 312 227-4464

Sat. & Sun. June 17 & 18: Marshall Antiques Market, Calhoun County Fairgrounds, Marshall. Sat. 8 to 4, Sun. 10 to 4. Admission: $3.00. 616 789-0990

Sunday June 25: Allegan Antique Market, Allegan Fairgrounds, Allegan. Sun. 7:30 to 4:30. 616 453-8780

JULY 1995

Wednesday July 4: Burley Park Antique & Collectible Market, Howard City. Mon. 8 to 4. Admission: $1.50. 616 354-6354

Sunday July 9: Caravan Antiques Market, Fairgrounds on Rt 86, Centerville. Sun. 7 to 4. Admission: $3.00. 312 227-4464

Sat. & Sun. July 15 & 16: Superfest Collectors Event, Ingham County Fairgrounds, Mason. Sat. 8 to 6, Sun. 9 to 4. Admission: $3.00. 517 676-2079

Sat. & Sun. July 15 & 16: Marshall Antiques Market, Calhoun County Fairgrounds, Marshall. Sat. 8 to 4, Sun. 10 to 4. Admission: $3.00. 616 789-0990

Sunday July 30: Allegan Antique Market, Allegan Fairgrounds, Allegan. Sun. 7:30 to 4:30. 616 453-8780

AUGUST 1995

Sunday August 6: Burley Park Antique & Collectible Market, Howard City. Mon. 8 to 4. Admission: $1.50. 616 354-6354

Sunday August 13: Caravan Antiques Market, Fairgrounds on Rt 86, Centerville. Sun. 7 to 4. Admission: $3.00. 312 227-4464

August 1995 - continued:
Sunday August 27: Allegan Antique Market, Allegan Fairgrounds, Allegan. Sun. 7:30 to 4:30. 616 453-8780

SEPTEMBER 1995

Monday September 4 (Labor Day): Burley Park Antique & Collectible Market, Howard City. Mon. 8 to 4. Admission: $1.50. 616 354-6354

Sat. & Sun. Sept. 9 & 10: Marshall Home Tour, with antique market at several locations. Sat. 9 to 5, Sun. 10 to 5. 616 781-5163

Sat. & Sun. September 16 & 17: Marshall Antiques Market, Calhoun County Fairgrounds, Marshall. Sat. 8 to 4, Sun. 10 to 4. Admission: $3.00. 616 789-0990

Sunday September 24: Allegan Antique Market, Allegan Fairgrounds, Allegan. Sun. 7:30 to 4:30. 616 453-8780

Mon. to Sun. September 25 to October 1: Meridian Mall, Lansing. 616 629-3133

OCTOBER 1995

Sunday October 1: Burley Park Antique & Collectible Market, Howard City. Mon. 8 to 4. Admission: $1.50. 616 354-6354

Sat. & Sun. October 7 & 8: Ford Fieldhouse, Grand Rapids. 616 629-3133

Sunday October 8: Caravan Antiques Market, Fairgrounds on Rt 86, Centerville. Sun. 7 to 4. Admission: $3.00. 312 227-4464

Sat. & Sun. October 14 & 15: Superfest Collectors Event, Ingham County Fairgrounds, Mason. Sat. 8 to 6, Sun. 9 to 4. Admission: $3.00. 517 676-2079

Sat. & Sun. October 14 & 15: Antique Show, Cook Energy Information Center, I-94 exit 16, 3 1/2 miles north on Red Arrow Highway, Bridgeman. Admission: FREE. 800 548-2555

Sat. & Sun. October 14 & 15: Marshall Antiques Market, Calhoun County Fairgrounds, Marshall. Sat. 8 to 4, Sun. 10 to 4. Admission: $3.00. 616 789-0990

Sat. & Sun. October 21 & 22: Collectors' Showcase, Stadium Arena, Grand Rapids. 616 629-3133

October 1995 - continued:
Sat. & Sun. October 28 & 29: The Barry Expo Center Antique Show, M-37 south from 28th St. SE and Woodland Mall, Middleville. Sat. 10 to 9, Sun. 10 to 6. Admission: $2.00. 616 453-8780.

NOVEMBER 1995

Sat. & Sun. November 25 & 26: Holiday Collectors' Showcase, Lansing Center, Lansing. 616 629-3133.

INDEX OF DEALER SPECIALTIES

Advertising:
4.1 14 Ward's Antiques, Allendale 96
9.3 13 Cherry Acres Antiques, Traverse City 163

Architectural Items:
2.1 10 Heritage Architectural Salvage, Klamazoo 50
2.3 6 Keystone Antiques, Marshall 56
2.4 8 Grand Illusion, Grass Lake 64

Art Deco:
3.4 9 Triola's, Lansing 84
4.2 8 All Era, Grand Rapids 100
10.4 3 Joseph's World Classic Antiques, Petoskey 176
10.4 26 DC-DOE Antiques, Oden 180

Beer Collectibles:
3.4 46 Things Beer, Williamston 90

Bells:
2.4 10 Brooklyn Depot Antiques, Brooklyn 65

Books:
1.1 39 Bibliotiques Antiques, Stevensville 23
1.2 4 Olympia Books and Prints, Dowagiac 29
1.4 6 Terry Farwell, Quincy 36
2.1 2 Hidden Room Book Shop, South Haven 44
10.1 7 Talponia Books Ltd., Alden 167
10.5 3 Books Etc., Indian River 184

Bottles:
1.1 24 Jeff's Trading Post, Sawyer 18

Copper Items:
11.14 9 Copper World, Calumet 211
11.15 13 The Museum Shop, Eagle Harbor 212

Country:
4.1 13 Maple Valley Antiques, Lamont 96
7.1 12 School House Antiques, Scottville 138
7.2 5 River Bend Trading Post, Baldwin 140
10.4 32 Little Bit Country, Levering 182

Dolls:
1.1 37 Mollie Zelmer Antiques, Buchanan 21
1.3 4 Collectibles Unlimited, Three Rivers 31
2.1 11 Lola's Doll Shoppe, Kalamazoo 50
2.3 20 Burlington Antiques & Collectibles, Burlington . . . 58
8.2 5 Antiques Unique, Manton 148
10.1 8 Dee's Antiques, Mancelona 168
10.4 23 Lee's Dolls, Cross Village 180

Index of Dealer Specialties - continued

Fifties:
1.1 17 Lakeside Antiques, Lakeside 17
1.1 21 Kalamazoo Antiques, Harbert 17
3.3 3 Best Wisches, Grand Ledge 79
3.3 5 Fifties & Such, Grand Ledge 79

Folk Art:
1.1 17 Lakeside Antiques, Lakeside 17
1.1 20 Global Dry Goods, Harbert 17
9.2 14 Back Roads Antiques, Northport 158

Furniture:
1.1 52 Good Old Times Antiques, Benton Harbor 26
1.1 58 Millstone Antique Shop, Coloma 27
1.6 6 Main Street Marketplace, Three Rivers 31
2.1 9 The Emporium, Kalamazoo 50
2.3 11 HilDor House Antiques, Marshall 57
2.4 1 Harley's Antique Mall, Parma (Albian) 60
2.4 4 The Jackson Antique Mall, Jackson 63
3.1 15 Tulip City Antique Mall, Holland 69
4.2 18 Flat River Antique Mall, Lowell 102
4.4 8 County Line Antiques, St. Johns 112
4.2 1 Greenville Antique Center, Greenville 117
6.2 7 R & E Variety, White Cloud 129
8.4 3 Houghton Lake Flea Market, Houghton Lake 151
9.3 10 Wilson Antiques, Traverse City 162
11.04 4 Christophers, Manistique 192

Furniture & House Hardware:
4.3 13 Robinson's Antiques, ... 108

Gas Station Memorabilia:
9.3 14 Walt's Antiques, Traverse City 163

Glassware:
1.1 40 Bill's Real Antiques, Stevensville 23
1.1 58 Millstone Antique Shop, Coloma 27
1.5 13 The Village Peddler, Allen 39
2.1 6 L & R Antiques, Lawrence 44
2.3 4 Heirlooms Unlimited, Marshall 56
2.4 22 Bailey's Antiques, Tekonsha 59
3.2 7 Daval's Used Furniture and Antiques 77
3.4 45 Old Village Antiques, Williamston 90
4.1 7 Patricia's Glass and Antiques, Grand Haven 95
4.2 12 Heirloom House Antiques, Grand Rapids 100
4.2 18 Flat River Antique Mall, Lowell 102
6.2 7 R & E Variety, White Cloud 129

Hoosier Cabinets:
1.1 24 Jeff's Trading Post, Sawyer 18

Index of Dealer Specialties - continued

Indian Artifacts:
1.1 11 Antique Mall & Village, Union Pier 15
1.1 29 Michiana Antique Mall, Niles 20
1.1 58 Millstone Antique Shop, Coloma 27
2.4 1 Harley's Antique Mall, Parma (Albian) 60
3.1 20 Plainwell Antiques, Plainwell 71
3.3 2 Bear Creek Trader, Potterville 79

Jewelry:
2.1 1 Anchor Antiques Ltd., South Haven 43
2.1 8 JP's Coins & Collectibles, Kalamazoo 50
3.4 32 Sally's Unique Jewelry & Antiques, Mason 88
3.4 52 Legends Jewelry, Williamston 91
4.2 18 Flat River Antique Mall, Lowell 102
11.07 2 Simply Charming, Menominee 198

Lighting:
3.4 9 Bohnet's, Lansing 84
9.3 3 Grey Wolf Antiques, Traverse City 160
10.5 5 Antiques & Collectibles, Cheboygan 184

Military:
1.2 1 Argus Antiques, Edwardsburg 28
2.1 13 Halsey Dean Gallery, Mattawan 46
2.4 5 The Antique Shop, Jackson 63
11.01 4 Superior Paper Company, St Ignace 187

Mission Oak:
1.1 11 Antique Mall & Village, Union Pier 15
1.1 14 East Road Gallery, Lakeside 15
1.5 15 Green Top Country Village, Allen 15
4.2 5 Antiques by the Bridge, Grand Rapids 99
4.2 7 Before & After Antiques, Grand Rapids 99
4.2 10 Heartwood, Grand Rapids 100
10.3 6 604 Bridge Antiques & Art, Charlevoix 172
10.3 7 Shop of All Crafters, Charlevoix 172

Music Boxes:
4.2 16 Turn of the Century Antiques, Grand Rapids 101

Musical Instruments:
1.1 11 Antique Mall & Village, Union Pier 15
2.1 6 Thieves Market, Kalamazoo 50
2.4 5 The Antique Shop, Jackson 63

Nautical Items:
11.01 3 Anchor In Antiques, St. Ignace 186

Oriental Rugs:
3.1 20 Plainwell Antiques, Plainwell 71

Index of Dealer Specialties - continued

Pine Furniture:
1.1 7 The Plum Tree, Union Pier 14
1.1 12 Rabbit Run, Lakeside 15
10.4 18 Pooter Olooms Antiques, Harbor Springs 179

Pottery:
1.1 21 Kalamazoo Antiques, Harbert 21
2.4 1 Harley's Antique Mall, Parma (Albion) 60
3.1 7 Tulip City Antique Mall, Holland 68
3.4 36 Tom Forshee Antiques, Stockbridge 89
7.2 8 Hopeful Antiques, Luther 141
10.4 30 Gaslight Antiques & Collectibles, Levering 181

Primitives:
1.1 42 Shawnee Road Antiques, Baroda 23
1.4 7 Raymond's Country Barn Antiques, Union City . . . 36
2.1 19 Holmes Antiques, Gobles 47
2.3 21 Kempton's Country Classics, Tekonsha 59
3.2 1 Hickory Hollow Antiques, Hickory Corners 75
7.2 1 Star Sales House, Baldwin 139

Radios and Phonographs:
5.3 5 Mac Lachlan House Antiques, Elwell 122

Repair & Refinishing:
4.2 17 Koning's Wood Products, Grand Rapids 101

Sporting Antiques:
1.3 7 Antoinette's Antiques, Three Rivers 32
3.4 5 The Antique Shop, Jackson 63
10.3 10 Wooden Duck Antiques, Charlevoix 173

Stamps:
2.3 20 Burlington Antiques & Collectibles, Burlington . . . 58

Tools:
1.1 58 Millstone Antique Shop 27
2.1 11 Tom Witte's Antiques, Mattawan 46
7.3 3 Good Friend's Antiques and Flea Market, Marion . . 142

Toys:
1.1 16 The Antique Complex, Lakeside 16
2.3 20 Burlington Antiques & Collectibles, Burlington . . . 58

Vintage Clothing:
2.2 1 Souk Sampler, Kalamazoo 48
3.4 24 The Garment District, Mason 86
4.2 9 A Scavenger Hunt, Grand Rapids 100
4.2 11 Nobody's Sweetheart Vintage, Grand Rapids 100